Vision

Vision

How Leaders Develop It,
Share It,
and Sustain It

Joseph V. Quigley
Quigley and Associates, Inc.

McGraw-Hill, Inc.

New York   San Francisco   Washington, D.C.   Auckland   Bogotá
Caracas   Lisbon   London   Madrid   Mexico City   Milan
Montreal   New Delhi   San Juan   Singapore
Sydney   Tokyo   Toronto

Library of Congress Cataloging-in-Publication Data

Quigley, Joseph V.
    Vision : how leaders develop it, share it, and sustain it /
Joseph V. Quigley.
        p.   cm.
    Includes index.
    ISBN 0-07-051084-9
    1. Leadership—Congresses. 2. Strategic planning—United States—
Congresses. 3. Leadership—Case studies—Congresses. 4. Strategic
planning—United States—Case studies—Congresses. I. Title.
HD57.7.Q55   1993
658.4′092—dc20   93-9582
                                                                        CIP

1 2 3 4 5 6 7 8 9 0   DOC/DOC   9 9 8 7 6 5 4 3

ISBN 0-07-051084-9

*The sponsoring editor for this book was James H. Bessent, Jr., the editing
supervisor was John Fitzpatrick of Editorial Services of New England, and the
production supervisor was Pamela A. Pelton. This book was set in Palatino by
McGraw-Hill's Professional Book Group composition unit.*

Printed and bound by R. R. Donnelley & Sons Company.

This book is printed on recycled, acid-free paper containing a
minimum of 50% recycled de-inked fiber.

To my wife, Jan,
who gave me love,
and to my mother and father,
who gave me life

Contents

Preface

The vision concept is highly topical. It has been on the agenda of the Conference Board's Annual Strategic Planning conference in each of the past two years. "The Vision Thing" was the topic of *Business Week*'s President's Forum. Yet, in my experience, not one in twenty corporations have what could pass as a vision statement inside or outside the company. Fewer than one in one hundred has a vision statement that has been effectively communicated to its people.

While vision has been discussed by other authors, there has been little definition of content. No one has described how to develop vision so that it has broad-based commitment. Equally important, there has been little written on how to communicate vision, how to renew it, and how to sustain it over long periods of time.

Vision is addressed to all those interested in the art of leadership and management, whether their interest is business or institutionally oriented, serious or casual. It is addressed not just to the leader but the leadership group, the board of directors, and those aspiring to join the group in either the near or long-term future.

This book should have particular appeal for those interested in the Malcolm Baldrige National Quality award. The process described for vision development provides a natural launching platform for total quality management (TQM). It can provide the heavy involvement of executive leadership necessary in establishing TQM as one of the major goals of the corporation.

Vision Precedes Strategy

For many years the leader's attention has been focused on *strategies*. There are myriad books on strategy, from strategies in Nintendo games to the strategy of marketing to the strategy of war. Strategies are directed toward achieving *goals,* but goals must flow out of the leader's *vision*. The question *Vision* addresses is: How do the leader and the leadership group formulate their fundamental *vision*?

This book gives a step-by-step description of how the leader and the leadership group can develop a distinctive corporate or institutional vision that creates shared ownership and commitment. The process I describe in this book is effective for any organization, whether it employs 200 people or 200,000.

Vision is generally the product of a group of leaders rather than the dream of an individual. It must contain both a challenge and a general road map showing how the organization will reach its goals.

The book goes well beyond *developing* the vision. It addresses how to *communicate* the vision, both short-term and long-term. Even a compelling vision requires effective communication to generate consensus and commitment beyond the small core group of authors.

Timely and consistent *stewardship* is critical to making the vision a reality. It is also critical to periodically *renew* the vision so that it retains vitality. This book recommends a stewardship process and emphasizes that, over the long term, leadership requires *sustained* vision and effective execution of supporting strategies.

The Structure of the Book

Part 1 of *Vision* examines the leader's vision as an answer to the search for meaning in our work and as the source of the leader's power and performance. It explores, defines, and gives examples of each element of the leader's vision: the values as the foundation of the vision; the mission as the fundamental statement of what the organization is today and what it aspires to be in the future; and the goals as setting the long-term direction of the organization. The relationship of the vision to the strategic plan is also briefly addressed.

Part 2 focuses on vision formation. It lays out in simple, practical steps how to develop vision, how to select the leadership group, and how to prepare the group for effective participation in the conferences the suggested process calls for. It then describes each of the suggested conferences in theme and format.

Part 3 discusses how to communicate the global vision throughout the organization by means of an effective "roll-out" process. It describes how to make the vision a reality through periodic review and renewal and gives a very specific description of the renewal process in action, a process important in maintaining the organization's vitality. Finally, it addresses whether a great corporation, like a great society, can sustain its vision, values, and vitality over time...or must inevitably lose its nerve and momentum.

Part 4 links the vision and values concepts, which are quite new and relatively undefined, to the older and better-understood concepts involved in the more traditional aspects of strategic planning. It establishes the corporate vision and shared values as the core of the leadership contract and the foundation of strategic planning. The final chapter examines organizational units other than the large corporation: the not-for profits, the family firm, and the intermediate and smaller company.

The Vision Process

A distinctive element about the process described in this book is that it is more collegial, consensus-, or group-oriented than other planning processes, which are more *personal* (individual- or leader-oriented) or *formal* (highly structured or hierarchical). As discussed in this book, a collegial or consensus process does not mean a democratic one. Listening to and respecting individual opinions are built into the process. But there are no votes unless the leader asks for one. The leader has the final responsibility and the final word.

Writing about Fortune 500 firms allowed me to focus on vision concepts and process as opposed to descriptions of a company or institution, its leaders, its market situation, and so forth. Fortune 500 firms clearly have high reader recognition, as do the situations they face in the marketplace.

The book lays out clearly and succinctly what the leader and leadership group can do to translate visionary concepts into action in any organization, profit or not-for-profit. It speaks directly to the leaders in a prescriptive style in the *"Rx for Leaders"* contained in each chapter. These are brief words of advice to the leader who wants to develop a compelling vision with a high degree of consensus, ownership, and commitment.

Many people associate the decade of the 1980s with greed, decadence, and erosion of values. The takeover "jockeys," their investment bankers, and lawyers see corporations as legal and paper entities to be bought, sold, traded, milked, liquidated, and disposed of. They do not

see the visions, the values, the dreams, the people, and the loyalties that
have inspired the builders of the world's biggest and best businesses.
This book is addressed to the business builders, not the buyers and sellers and their money center bankers.

Joseph V. Quigley

Acknowledgments

The CEOs I worked for in my corporate career were most significant in shaping my views on the leader's vision and values. The first and by far most important was Tom Watson, Jr., who became CEO the year I joined IBM and retired the year I resigned. He and his father personified my view of the leader. Other CEOs who shaped my thinking while I worked for and with them were Bob Dee at Smith Kline, Robert Sarnoff at RCA, and Bob Baldwin at Gulf Oil.

Client CEOs that I have worked with closely over the last 15 years have also made a significant contribution to my thinking. They include Bill Ruckelshaus at Browning-Ferris Industries, Fred Stratton at Briggs & Stratton, Jim Chapman and Charlie Strang at Outboard Marine Corporation, Pete Silas at Phillips Petroleum, Jerry Castiglia at Pratt & Lambert Paint Company, and Archabbot Timothy Sweeney, OSB at St. Meinrad Archabbey.

Several people made significant contributions to the manuscript itself through their comments, critiques, or suggestions. They include Tom Liptak, formerly vice president of organization and management systems at IBM; Neil Miller of Gulf Oil; Art Gechman of Personnel Decisions, Inc.; Sister Mary Margaret Funk, Prioress of Our Lady of Grace Monastery; and Jim O'Mahoney, a friend from my grade school days. Al Calabria and James O'Brien of Quigley & Associates were also heavy contributors.

There were also a group of "promoters," enthusiasts who offered support at many different stages of development. They include friends, clients, and associates: Tom Beeler and Bob Randolph at Outboard Marine Corporation; Scott Carlberg, Bill Wertz, and Brian Whitworth at

Phillips Petroleum; Jim Hennessy at NYNEX; Ski Hilenski of the University of South Carolina; Monsignor McCabe of the Diocese of Austin, Texas; Tom Quilter of the Planning Forum; Buck Rodgers, formerly Vice President of Marketing at IBM; as well as Vern Brisson, Chris Christy, Dan Conway, Dick Kirkely, Jerry Puls, Carl Stevens, Joe Synan, Phil Taggart, Ken Thoren and Ford Worthing. My brothers and sister, Dan, Mike, and Kitty, were also among the promoters. But my biggest promoter was my brother, Jerry, who supported me in many ways and was always looking for other ways.

My biggest debt is to my wife, Jan, who has supported me through this whole project and my whole life both lovingly and unselfishly. I am also indebted to my mother and father for the sense of values they instilled in me and the sense of vision they encouraged. This appreciation of vision, values, and leadership was much enhanced by the priests and teachers at St. Meinrad Archabbey in southern Indiana.

Books are not published without a massive amount of direct help in typing, proofing, suggesting, and encouraging. I am most indebted to my daughter, Beth Benefield, who saw the project start and finish and was always at my side in between. Susan Garret offered much help and enthusiasm in the early stages as did another daughter, Molly.

Finally, I thank my editor, Jim Bessent, and my agent, Meredith Bernstein, for their faith in me as a first-time author and for kindly showing me the way. Thanks also to Elisa Adams, whose review and comments added immeasurably to the quality of the book.

Special Thanks

We would like to thank the following companies who have contributed to the knowledge base from which this book has been created:

American Capital Management & Research, Inc.

American Management Association

American Medical International

Baker International Corporation

Banc One

Brazos Valley Symphony Orchestra

Briggs & Stratton

Brown & Root

Browning-Ferris Industries (BFI)

Coleman Company

Combustion Engineering

Cooper Industries

Daniel Industries

Federal Aviation Administration

Gulf Oil

HEI Corporation

Halliburton Company

Harrisburg, Inc.

Hertz

Houston Economic Development Council

Houston Forum Club

Houston Grand Opera

IBM

Lawn-Boy

Louisiana Tech University

Lufkin Industries

McCoy, Inc.

Midcon

NBC

Outboard Marine Corporation

Periodical Management Group

Personnel Decision, Inc.

Phillips Petroleum

Pratt & Lambert

RCA

RWR Enterprises

Ralston Purina

Republic Gypsum Company

Sentry Insurance

Shell Oil

Sisters of Charity Health Care System

Smith International

SmithKline Beckman

Southwestern Bell

St. Meinrad Archabbey

Texas A&M University

Texas State Department of Highways

Texas Woman's University

Titleist

Twin Disc

United Energy

United States Air Force

University of South Carolina

University of Texas at Austin

Vetco

Warren Petroleum

A Special Acknowledgment of Endorsers

The vast majority of books on leadership have been written *by* academics *for* academics. For instance, in his fine book, *On Becoming a Leader*, Warren Bennis says he writes for "my 'invisible college' of intellectual giants who always flatter me by reading and commenting on my efforts, John Gardner, James MacGregor Burns, David Riesman, and Peter Drucker."

This book is written for a distinctly different audience, namely, current and aspiring *leaders*, by an active consultant in visioning and strategic planning. Many of these leaders were given an advance look at this book, and as a lead-in to their generous comments, I would like to thank them one and all for their support and endorsement of my efforts. They are or have been active leaders in their own right, and their endorsements reflect broad interest in the vision and values theme from leaders of major corporations, public figures, institutional and religious leaders, as well as leaders of intermediate and smaller corporations.

Kenneth Blanchard, author of *The One-Minute Manager*, calls them "an incredible group of endorsements." I would just add that it's also an incredible group of endorsers. Many thanks.

"CEOs and aspirants alike will find *Vision* an invaluable tool....I highly recommend it as a road map for those who guide their institutions into the future."

> *Robert W. Baldwin*
> *President & CEO, Gulf Refining &*
> *Marketing (Ret.)*

"*Vision* is good medicine for private sector management, but will also go a long way to educate and inspire public servants at all levels of government."

> *Evan Bayh*
> *Governor of Indiana*

"The concepts and procedures described in *Vision* were indispensable in developing teamwork and resolve to put our strategy into action."

> *J. J. Castiglia*
> *President & CEO, Pratt & Lambert*

"Joe Quigley, in *Vision,* captures the mood of the 1990s. This book must be read if you are intending to have an impact in the next decade."

> *Robert L. Dilenschneider*
> *Former President and CEO,*
> *Hill and Knowlton*

"For years *Chief Executive* has championed the global vision as prerequisite of companies today.... To the extent that this book can dispel the artificial distinction too often made between 'business' and 'international business' in the minds of today's managers (and politicians), it will serve a worthy cause."

> *J.P. Donlon*
> *Editor, Chief Executive Magazine*

"The substance of the issues addressed in *Vision* is important to all leaders and to those who would be leaders. I commend Joe Quigley for his insights."

> *Thomas Ehrlich*
> *President, Indiana University*

"Religious CEOs would profit from this book. We steward enormous resources for the People of God. Seldom does anyone teach with such authority as does Joe Quigley in his *Vision*."

Mary Margaret Funk, O.S.B.,
Prioress, Our Lady of Grace Monastery

"Your book takes the giant step from philosophy to implementation. It is not just a collection of good advice. It creates a very strategic path for people to follow to create stronger organizations."

Patricia Hayes, Ph.D.,
President, St. Edwards University

"The world today, especially the business world, desperately needs leadership which is founded on Vision and Values. *Vision* is a powerful tool both to develop and to sustain such leadership."

Theodore M. Hesburgh, C.S.C.
President Emeritus, University of Notre Dame

"*Vision* sets forth a highly participative planning process for developing an organization's vision and values. The process started as a corporate model. But, with adaptation, it is equally effective in a church or institutional setting. It worked extremely well for us."

Thomas C. Kelly, O.P.
Archbishop, Archdiocese of Louisville

"Regarding your new book, *Vision,* both the topic and your analysis and course of action seem to me to be right on target. A mission without values is like a journey without a road map. I am confident that it will not only be well received but widely used."

Leo E. Linbeck, Jr.
CEO, Linbeck Construction Corporation .

"Very readable....*Vision* is unique, differentiating and value added....This book should be read by present and future leaders and I don't restrict this statement to industry people."

Thomas M. Liptak
Corporate V.P., Organization and
Management Systems, IBM (Ret.)

"Congratulations to Joe Quigley. After the excesses of the eighties, it was past time that someone remind us of the importance of values in determining corporate success or failure. Better yet, with this book the message comes...from a seasoned and successful practitioner."

Edward A. Malloy, C.S.C.
President, University of Notre Dame

"Your approach is common sense, based on significant experience in the world of corporate planning....My experience as a leader seems to match what you stress: sense of vision, listening, shared effort in values and planning, and mixed with good common sense."

Joseph McFadden
President, University of St. Thomas

"There has never been a time when the message of *Vision* is as important as it is today. While values never change, flexibility and leadership are important. *Vision*'s message points the way."

Andrew J. McKenna
CEO, Schwarz Paper Company,
Chairman of the Board of Trustees,
University of Notre Dame

"*Vision* focuses on large companies with high name recognition. But the leadership process described is both more critical and more easily translated into action in smaller companies. I know. I have worked for both. Small companies can't afford mistakes. A faulty vision can put us out of business."

Thad Minyard
President & CEO, McCoy, Inc.

"In *Vision* Joe Quigley encourages us to think about ourselves as leaders. In so doing, he causes us to ask important questions about ourselves and our roles—and thus he makes us better leaders."

Roy A. Nicholson
Chairman & CEO, USA Funds, Inc.

"Your book visualizes for leaders a path that defines current reality globally and a process to go beyond the limits to creative possibilities."

Sister Carmella O'Donoghue, President
& CEO, Sisters of Charity of the
Incarnate Word Health Care System

"I subscribe to the theory and process delineated in *Vision* and will make it mandatory reading for my managers....Your statement that, 'This book is addressed to the business builders, not the buyers and sellers and their bankers,' will stimulate the reader to read on."

Robert D. Randolph
COO and Executive V.P., Outboard Marine
Corporation

"*Vision* is a most timely antidote to the widespread concern about the leadership vacuum in American society today. The principles clearly delineated by Joe Quigley are applicable in every type of institution— governmental, business, educational, and philanthropic."

Paul C. Reinert, S.J.
Chancellor Emeritus, Saint Louis University

"Vision is not just important...it is crucial to any organization achieving consistent and sustainable superior performance. *Vision* gives real and practical insights on how to inoculate your organization with it."

Wolfgang R. Schmitt
Co-chairman of the Board & CEO,
Rubbermaid Incorporated

"This book contains fundamental skills necessary for successful management. Nothing is more important than top management's vision and values in determining what happens in an organization. It is the basis for all other management skills and practices. This book could easily have been titled 'Vision and Values: What Every Manager *Must* Know About Them.' I strongly recommend this book for top managers of both private and public organizations."

George A. Steiner
Kunin Professor of Business and
Society, and Professor of
Management (Emeritus), UCLA

"Just as Ronald Reagan succeeded in refocusing America on becoming the shining city on the hill...so too does *Vision* give us the incentive and the method by which we...can focus on our own shining cities. The author encourages us to set our goals, select wisely, be prepared for competition, and in the end, achieve success. I commend this book to your reading."

George W. Strake, Jr.
Former Secretary of State, Texas, Chairman
and CEO, Strake Trading Group

"From personal experience in working with Joe Quigley, I know that *Vision* raises the right questions for an institution and shows the path for a leader to explain the vision and to elicit implementation and accountability."

Timothy Sweeney, O.S.B.,
Archabbot, St. Meinrad Archabbey

"We had the good fortune to use the methods discussed in *Vision* before they were part of this book. Of all the many benefits team building and 'buy-in' were truly the best."

C. Richard Vermillion, Jr.
Chairman & CEO, Banc One, Texas NA

"*Vision* consolidates the actual leadership conference planning process into a clear, concise, step-by-step guide which will prove invaluable to any CEO desiring to foster team commitment, ownership, and esprit de corps within their organization."

D. H. Waldschmitt
President and CEO, Harrisburg, Inc.

"*Vision* shows how your organization can create vision, instill values, and develop a strategic plan that is aligned to both. I found the book enjoyable and thought provoking."

Marcia Worthing
Senior V. P., Human Resources,
Avon Products, Inc.

"*Vision* addresses…a critical difference between an ethical or *value*-focused leader and one who simply runs an organization.…"

William H. Zierdt, III
Director, Corporate Consulting,
International Values Institute

PART 1

Elements of the Leader's Vision and Values

- Establishes the leader's vision as the fundamental source of power.
- Emphasizes the leader's responsibility for the basic elements of the vision.
- Defines and gives examples of corporate values—the most fundamental element of the vision.
- Breaks down the mission statement into its subelements.
- Defines goals with additional examples.
- Reviews strategies and tactics as the action steps that move the organization toward vision realization.

1
Vision

The Fundamental Source of Power

Life is a process of competition and selection, and leaders understand this. Leaders compete for the minds and hearts of those who would join or follow them. A leader's vision implies an understanding of the past and present. More importantly, it offers a road map to the future and suggests guidelines to those in a given enterprise—how they are to act and interact to attain what they regard as desirable. A leader's vision may be intuitive or highly structured. But it is the bedrock for success in meeting the twin tests of competition and selection.

Some of the earliest and strongest visions were religious in nature. The vision of Buddha, Moses, Christ, and Mohammed still compel followers throughout the world.

National Visions

The peoples of leading nations have always had a strong sense of vision. Sixteen years after the end of World War II, John Gardner laid out what he called the "shared aims of a free people," or his view of the American vision: peace with justice, freedom, the dignity and worth of the individual, the opportunity for every person to achieve the best that is in him or her, and equality before the law.[1] Gardner points out that this list is not exhaustive, but it is certainly indicative of the shared values of the American people.

[1]John W. Gardner, *Excellence*, Harper & Row, New York, 1961, pp. 155–156.

Neither leaders nor followers are always able to move in a straight line toward the achievement of their vision. Lincoln Kirstein, artistic director of the New York City Ballet, when commenting on his namesake, Abraham Lincoln, said, "We see the Lincolnian self, capable of delay, double-talk, maneuver, hesitancy, compromise, in order that one prime aim of his own era be effected: preservation of Federal union."[2]

Global Visions

Global visions that go beyond the religious or national visions have captured the imagination of many. One such vision was defined at the eleventh World Management Congress, held by the World Management Council at the Waldorf Astoria Hotel in New York City. Council board members included David Rockefeller, Peter Drucker, John Gardner, David Packard, Frank Stanton, and Tom Watson, Jr. The Congress was attended by members of approximately 50 nations, including Russia.

The theme of the Congress was "Management Challenges for the 1990s." Most of the speakers and panel members were a veritable *Who's Who* of corporate management, such as Bob Anderson, former CEO of ARCO, and Jack Kuehler, president of IBM. Another group included Henry Kravis, Boone Pickens, Carl Icahn, and Jesse Jackson. The importance of the Congress was indicated by a message from the pope, who asked the business people convened to reaffirm their business ethics, focus on the people they manage, and keep in mind the needs of the third world.

The opening session of the Congress included a keynote speech by Mortimer Adler, noted author and philosopher. Adler sees the major issue facing the world as singular and foreboding—the viability of human life on planet earth. In his opinion, the global environment problem must be solved early in the next century or we will not be here 100 years from today. To address this global environment problem, he has *a vision of a worldwide cultural community, or transcultural community.*

Adler indicated that some progress had already been made toward this end. He cited first the leading corporations of the world that are now supranational. The second indicator of transcultural progress he cited was technology. For Adler technology represents the westernizing of the globe and the greatest institutional innovation of the century, and frequently it is the offspring of these same leading corporations.

Adler's vision is not a dream. It represents a continuing evolution of the corporation that began in the twentieth century. Drucker says "on the performance of these institutions, the performance of modern soci-

---

[2]Warren Bennis and Burt Nanus, *Leaders: The Strategies for Taking Charge,* Harper & Row, New York, 1985, p. 31, with permission.

ety—if not the survival of each individual—increasingly depends....Business management is one of the very few institutions capable of transcending national boundaries."[3]

The Corporation as an Institution

Philosophers and historians have really only begun to assess the role of the large supranational corporation in the western world. A brief comparison to other major institutions such as the church, state, and family is appropriate. Churches in the western world are struggling to remain vital and to keep their members actively involved. They are fortunate to receive an hour a week from most of their members. The nation and state get even less of our time directly. While our tax bite may be large, we pay our taxes by mail, and thus we seldom come into direct contact with our state or nation as an institution. The role of the family in our society also seems to be declining. The typical family has become highly mobile, and its members are often preoccupied, with significant interactions limited to an evening meal, if that.

The corporation, on the other hand, is the focal point of many people's lives for 40 to 60 hours per week. It is the institution that they have the most contact with and the one they are most familiar with.

An effective case can be made for the significant role the corporation has played in post–World War II peace among the developed nations. A corporation's suppliers today are often global in scope, and their markets and customers are widely distributed. It is not customary for corporations to wage war with their suppliers or customers. One must treat them with care and respect, as partners in success. When the Berlin Wall finally came tumbling down as a symbol of division between East and West, between communism and capitalism, it was the same supranational corporations—IBM, GM, GE, and PepsiCo—that moved in immediately and closed the first big deals. To better appreciate the size of these supranational corporations, realize that their annual budgets surpass those of most member countries of the United Nations.

The Corporate Vision

The corporate vision is the most fundamental statement of a corporation's values, aspirations, and goals. It is an appeal to its members' hearts and minds. It must indicate a clear understanding of where the

[3]Peter F. Drucker, *Management: Tasks, Practices, Responsibilities,* Harper & Row, New York, 1973, pp. 3, 10.

corporation is today and offer a road map for the future. Because the corporation is so very important in our lives, we as members want to know:

- What distinctive or fundamental beliefs
  the corporation stands for ➤ VALUES
- What it is today and what it aspires to be ➤ MISSION
- What it is committed to and where it is going ➤ GOALS

The answers to these questions form the essential elements of the vision, with shared values as the foundation. The vision should be viewed as open- rather than close-ended. This definition is not intended to exclude the leader's creativity. But the fundamental vision question must be answered in a way that stimulates the organization. The next few chapters will explore the answers to these three basic questions.

Some will argue that profit, not vision, is the primary corporate motivator. But profit alone is not enough to motivate people. In fact, profit is perceived negatively by many people in corporations. Employees often see profit as something they earn, which management then takes and passes on to shareholders. While this perception may be distressing to management, it clearly indicates that twin motivators—profit *and* vision—are required to get the most out of a corporation's people.

Although employees may not understand profit or may even be alienated by the notion of profit, almost all will buy into the concepts of customer service, superior quality, integrity, and excellence if the corporation as a whole makes a serious effort to live up to these values. A statement of *vision* must be provided by the leaders of the corporation, particularly the CEO, because "A business corporation is not only an economic entity but a community, possibly the central community of our times....What the leader hopes to do is to unite the people in the organization into a 'responsible community'."[4]

Vision as the Key Leadership Attribute

Korn/Ferry International recently reported on a survey of 1500 senior leaders, 870 of them CEOs, from 20 different countries,[5] including representatives from Japan, the United States, Western Europe, and Latin

[4]Warren Bennis and Burt Nanus, *Leaders*, p. 211.

[5]Lester B. Korn, "How the Next CEO will be Different", *Fortune*, May 22, 1989, p. 157, with permission.

America. The leaders were asked to describe the key traits or talents desirable for a CEO today and important for a CEO in the year 2000. The dominant personal behavior trait most frequently mentioned, both for now and expected in the year 2000, was that the CEO convey a "strong sense of vision" (see Fig. 1-1). A rather amazing 98 percent saw that trait as most important for the year 2000. When the leaders were asked to cite key knowledge and skills for CEOs of the present and future, "strategy formulation" to achieve a vision was seen as the most important skill for now and in the year 2000, by a margin of 25 percent over any other skill.

Some executives see the scope of their vision more broadly than others. Business leaders in the United States are accustomed to the separation of church, state, and corporation. They generally assume the mandate of the corporation to be economic only. Japanese leaders see the role of corporations much more broadly, involving personal, family, social, and civil aspects of their employees' lives. Consequently, their corporate visions are much broader and are often seen as stronger. Americans seem to perceive this as an asset in Japan's favor. In a recent poll conducted by Louis Harris & Associates, Inc. for *Business Week,* 64 percent of Americans felt that the U.S. economy will be dominated by foreign companies over the next 10 years, and they had special concern about the Japanese.[6]

Rx for Leaders No. 1   Make your vision as clear as your profit goals. Profit alone is not enough to motivate your people. Expand the scope of your vision to address more of the whole person.

The Employee's Rights and Obligations

The employee's rights go further than the right to fair pay and fair treatment. Max DePree, chairman of Herman Miller, a manufacturer of quality office furniture and partitions and the smallest company ever to be selected to *Fortune* magazine's "Most Admired Companies," speaks of the rights of employees without distinction as to level or stature in the organization:

These rights are essential if there is to be a new concept of work. It is not a complete list of rights, of course, but these eight are essential:

The right to be needed

---

[6]"How Americans Feel About Their Future", *Business Week,* September 25, 1989, p. 175.

WHAT TRAITS CEOs HAVE–AND WILL NEED

Percent describing traits or talents dominant now in the CEO and important for the CEO of 2000

PERSONAL BEHAVIOR	NOW	YEAR 2000
Conveys strong sense of vision	75%	98%
Links compensation to performance	66%	91%
Communicates frequently with employees	59%	89%
Emphasizes ethics	74%	85%
Plans for management succession	56%	85%
Communicates frequently with customers	41%	78%
Reassigns or terminates unsatisfactory employees	34%	71%
Reward loyalty	48%	44%
Makes all major decisions	39%	21%
Behaves conservatively	32%	13%

KNOWLEDGE AND SKILLS	NOW	YEAR 2000
Strategy Formulation	68%	78%
Human resource management	41%	53%
International economics and politics	10%	19%
Science and technology	11%	15%
Computer literacy	3%	7%
Marketing and sales	50%	48%
Negotiation	34%	24%
Accounting and finance	33%	24%
Handling media and public speaking	16%	13%
Production	21%	9%

Increasing in importance ☐ Decreasing in importance

✳ More than 75% in the year 2000

Fortune
May 22, 1989, p. 157

Figure 1-1 Traits CEOs have and will need. Percent describing traits or talents dominant now in the CEO and important for the CEO of 2000. (*From Lester B. Korn, "How the Next CEO will be different," Fortune, May 22, 1989, p. 175, with permission.*)

The right to be involved
The right to a covenantal relationship
The right to understand
The right to affect one's own destiny
The right to be accountable
The right to appeal
The right to make a commitment.[7]

The leader must provide an answer to the search for corporate meaning by everyone in the organization. That answer must be provided by the leader's vision.

In exploring employees' rights, it is appropriate to consider employees' obligations as well. What are the obligations of employees in a corporation without distinctions as to level or stature? Bob Baldwin, former CEO of Gulf Refining and Marketing in Houston, Texas, has identified several. In his view, just as the employee has the right to respect as an individual, there is a corresponding obligation to respect the work group and the corporation as a whole. Employees have a right to a covenantal relationship, but as a part of that relationship they carry the corresponding obligation of loyalty and confidentiality to both their immediate and larger work group. To complement the employee's right to make a commitment and be held accountable, there is a corresponding obligation to the work group and employer to actually make that commitment and be held accountable for it. Finally, employees have the right to be needed, to use their gifts, and, at the same time, an obligation to use those gifts to the extent of their ability on behalf of their work group and employer.

Rx for Leaders No. 2 Define and respect your peoples' rights. Make certain they also understand their obligations to their work group and the organization. Both perspectives are needed.

Government and Public Service Institutions

This chapter has addressed vision primarily from a corporate perspective. Government and public service institutions have no less a need for vision and shared values. The government and public service sector account for well over 50 percent of the U.S. gross national product (GNP).

---

[7]Max DePree, *Leadership is an Art*, Doubleday, New York, 1989, pp. 31–36, with permission.

In other parts of the world, the proportion is much higher. If Peter Drucker is correct in his statement that modern society depends upon the performance of large institutions for its very survival, the government and public service sectors take on even greater significance.

The meaning of an employee's task can be easily lost in large governmental and public service institutions. But the search for meaning always remains, and the vision of the enterprise must provide that meaning. Since the monetary reward that an employee receives from government and public service institutions may be smaller, the vision must be even more compelling. Like Japanese corporations, these institutions must address much more of the whole person than their domestic corporate counterparts. For all of these reasons, the contents of this chapter and this book as a whole apply to the government and public service sectors as well as to the business sector.

The Leader's Vision as the Source of Power

The leader who offers a clear vision that is both coherent and credible, and who lives by a set of values that inspire imitation, has a fundamental source of power. Power can be defined as "the ability to get things done, to mobilize resources, to get and use whatever it is that a person needs for the goals he or she is attempting to meet."[8] This is an excellent working definition of power for operating people in an organization. A broader definition of power is "the basic energy to initiate and sustain action translating intention into reality,"[9] or put another way, "the capacity to translate intention into reality and sustain it." This definition is more appropriate for the visionary, the leader, the CEO. Working from that definition, I contend that *a leader's power is the capacity to translate a vision and supporting values into reality and sustain them.*

The first definition looks at power in terms of the structures and processes of the corporation, essentially from an inside perspective. The latter definition—and the one that I am advocating—recognizes a corporation's internal constituencies, i.e., managers, employees, and so forth, but it also looks at the corporation's other constituencies, i.e., the board, the shareholders, the customers, and the suppliers.

---

[8]Rosabeth Moss Kanter, *Men and Women of the Corporation,* Basic Books, New York, 1977, p. 166, with permission.

[9]Bennis and Nanus, *Leaders,* pp. 15, 17.

Empowering Others

Power flows from vision. The leader's power is suboptimized unless it empowers others. "The leader arouses confidence in his followers. The followers feel better able to accomplish whatever goals he and they share."[10] The leader *pulls* rather than *pushes* people on.

At the World Management Congress mentioned earlier, quality through empowered people was seen as one of the twin pillars of future corporate success. The other pillar was "servant leadership." Robert Greenleaf, author of *Servant Leadership*, explains this further in a comparison between servant power and coercive power: "In a complex institution-centered society, which ours is likely to be into the indefinite future, there will be large and small concentrations of power. Sometimes it will be a servant's power of persuasion and example.

Sometimes it will be coercive power used to dominate and manipulate people. The difference is that, in the former, power is used to create opportunity and alternatives so that the individuals may choose and build autonomy. In the latter, individuals are coerced into a predetermined path."[11]

Power Must Result in Performance

Ultimately, a leader's vision-based power must result in superior competitive performance. This is not a wish or desire; it is an imperative. Speaking of society at large and the individual in particular, John Gardner makes the point both more expansively and more personally: "Our society cannot achieve greatness unless individuals at many levels of ability accept the need for high standards of performance and strive to achieve those standards...."[12]

Holding high standards of performance means expecting to be the best. A leader's power can be maintained and enhanced only through performance, that is, through progress toward achieving the goals implied in the leader's vision.

For a number of years there was little empirical evidence that a firm with a strong sense of vision and shared values also demonstrated superior performance in the marketplace. That evidence has now been

[10]Thomas J. Peters and Robert H. Waterman Jr. , *In Search of Excellence,* HarperCollins Publishers , New York, 1982, p. 84, with permission.

[11]Robert K. Greenleaf, *Servant Leadership,* Paulist Press, Mahwah New Jersey, 1979, pp. 41–42, with permission.

[12]Gardner, *Excellence,* p. 131.

supplied by Harvard Business School professors John Kotter and James Heskett in their new book *Corporate Culture and Performance.* In a 4-year study concluded last year that focused on 9 to 10 firms in each of 20 industries, they found that firms with a strong corporate culture, based on a foundation of shared values, outperformed the other firms by a huge margin. The cultures of the winning firms placed emphasis on three key constituencies: customers, employees, and shareholders. The differences in performance in the two sets of companies is summarized below.

	Average growth for firms with performance-enhancing culture (%)	Average growth for firms without performance-enhancing culture
Revenue	682	166
Employment	282	36
Stock Price	901	74
Profit	756	1

The Kotter and Heskett argument is quantitatively supported and by no means simplistic. It emphasizes that a strong corporate culture alone is not enough. It must be combined with an appropriate business strategy for the given industry. This strong and strategically appropriate culture must be combined with a highly adaptive approach to change in the external world. A final and necessary ingredient is strong leadership at all levels of the organization, not just at the top.

Kotter and Heskett also found that weaker corporate cultures can be made more performance-enhancing, although the task is difficult and of long duration. Only leaders can effect these changes.

Rx for Leaders No. 3   Make sure your vision and values address all vital constituents: the customers, your people, and the shareholders. The customer always comes first.

Superior Performance Requires Superior Rewards.   Superior performance calls for superior rewards. Both the organization and the individuals in it seek rewards, but they need to be treated separately. In addition to monetary rewards, an individual's rewards include a sense of confidence and worth and a sense of what's good and bad for the organization, which helps the employee with decisions that might otherwise be difficult. "When the organization has a clear sense of its purpose, direction, and desired future state, and when this image is widely shared, individuals are able to find their own roles."[13] If top industry performance is achieved, the corporation should not be the only one that benefits financially. In addition to the sense of purpose, direction, and worth gained by the employees, their compensation should also be the highest in the industry. In short, their pay should be proportionate to their performance.

The corporation also seeks its rewards. It tries to maximize its reward from its *relative* position in the external environment. It must always see itself as part of the competitive world, setting its goals and tracking its performance in terms of its relative or competitive position in the marketplace. Profit is the first and most immediate reward. Profit is the market's measure of how the firm is valued. But the lasting reward for clearly superior competitive performance is enhanced power in the marketplace, or market power. In the final analysis, the most fundamental determinant of business success is the customer's perception of a corporation's product or service relative to its competitors. This is not only more basic and more lasting than profit, it is the determinant of profit.

Rx for Leaders No. 4   Increase your market power and profitability by improving your customer's perception of your product or service relative to your competitors. This perception is the leading indicator of corporate strategic health. Profit is a trailing indicator.

The Top Performers.   The top performers in the U.S. Fortune 500 generally place emphasis on all the key constituencies of customer, employee, and shareholder emphasized by professors Kotter and Heskett. While there are many ways and numerous criteria for identifying top performers, one such process surveys 8000 senior executives, outside directors, and financial analysts to determine *Fortune*'s "Most Admired Companies." Each year since 1983, these leaders have selected their 10 most admired corporations. Even companies that have only been selected once generally possess strong power in their selected markets.

---

[13]Bennis and Nanus, *Leaders*, p. 90.

They include AT&T, Digital Equipment, General Mills, DuPont, Eli Lilly, RJR Nabisco, Smithkline Beecham, and Time Inc.

Those that have been selected twice include the smallest company ever selected, Herman Miller, the furniture manufacturer mentioned earlier with less than a billion dollars in annual sales. Others include Eastman Kodak, Exxon, and Shell Oil. Those selected three times represent an even higher level of performance and market dominance. They include Anheuser-Busch, General Electric, Hewlett-Packard, J.P. Morgan, Liz Claiborne, PepsiCo, and Philip Morris. Those elected four or more times vary greatly in size, but each company is truly a top performer. Their market power is almost epic in their industry. They include Boeing, Coca-Cola, Dow Jones, IBM, Johnson & Johnson, Merck, Procter and Gamble, Rubbermaid, 3M, and Wal-Mart.

The founders of a few of these companies are still living. In others, the vision and values of the founders have been nurtured by successor CEOs and leadership groups. More than a few have gone through difficult periods since their inclusion in the *Fortune* list. But the vast majority have kept their vision fresh and their values stable through changing times.

Of course, not all companies win the battle for survival. The mortality rate is very high. One-third of the Fortune 500 companies listed in 1970 were gone by 1983. And the pace of mortality has accelerated. Of the 500 corporations listed in 1983, almost 30 percent have already vanished. If there had been no additions since 1970, the Fortune 500 would now be the Fortune 167.

Rx for Leaders No. 5   Develop a performance-enhancing culture in your company. Remember that the corporate mortality rate is approaching 6 percent a year, and the pace is quickening.

2

Values

The Foundation of Vision

In *The Lessons of History,* Will and Ariel Durant say that "morals are the rules by which a society exhorts (as laws are the rules by which it seeks to compel) its members and associations to behavior consistent with its order, security, and growth."[1] Paraphrasing the Durants, I define corporate values as *the rules or guidelines by which a corporation exhorts its members to behavior consistent with its order, security, and growth.* As a corporation becomes an institution, and thus a society in itself, a set of values and beliefs becomes a necessity.

Values and beliefs are the most fundamental of the three elements of vision. Founders possess an established set of values at the time they give birth to an enterprise, generally long before they develop even an informal mission statement or set of goals. Values precede mission and goals in logic and reality. Consequently, primacy in the corporate vision is shifting from corporate mission to corporate values.

Early Research on Corporate Values

Values and beliefs as a component of the corporate vision statement are relatively new on the American business scene. They have not been made explicit in most corporations and many leaders feel uncertain in

[1]Will and Ariel Durant, *The Lessons of History,* Simon & Schuster, New York, 1968, p. 37.

this area. There has been considerable research regarding values over the last 25 years.

For example, in 1977, five years prior to their publication of *In Search of Excellence,* Thomas J. Peters and Bob Waterman wrote about superordinate goals in *Business Horizons,* which they describe as, "a set of values and aspirations, often unwritten, that goes beyond the conventional formal statement of corporate objectives. Superordinate goals are the fundamental ideas around which a business is built. They are its main values."[2] Subsequently, McKinsey made superordinate goals part of the its "Seven S" framework, the fundamental elements of all corporations. The other six are *strategy, structure, systems, style, staff, and skills.* Superordinate goals were seen as sort of a first among equals, playing a very central role among the other S's.

Superordinate goals must be succinct if they are to be communicated effectively. They are often expressed quite abstractly. To outsiders who are not familiar with the organization, they may seem ordinary or mundane. To insiders, however, they are very significant and have a strong emotional appeal.

The topic of values also received attention by Richard Pascale and Anthony Athos in *The Art of Japanese Management* (1978). They defined superordinate goals as "the overarching purposes to which an organization and its members dedicate themselves."[3] Rarely are they bottom-line secular goals like x percent growth or y percent return on investment. Rather, they pertain to values or goals that "move people's hearts." The authors go on to point out that the most effective superordinate goals must be (1) significant, (2) durable, and (3) achievable.

What Values Do Excellent Companies Hold?

In *In Search of Excellence,* Peters and Waterman found the specific content of the dominant beliefs of the companies they profiled to be narrow in scope, including just a few basic values, namely:

1. A belief in being the "best"
2. A belief in the importance of the details of execution, the nuts and bolts of doing the job well

[2]Robert H. Waterman, Jr., Thomas J. Peters, and Julien R. Phillips, "Structure Is not Organization", *Business Horizons,* June 1980, pp. 24–25.

[3]Richard T. Pascale and Anthony G. Athos, *The Art of Japanese Management,* Simon & Schuster, New York, 1981, pp. 81–82.

3. A belief in the importance of people as individuals

4. A belief in superior quality and service

5. A belief that most members of the organization should be innovators, as well as the belief in its corollary, a willingness to support failure

6. A belief in the importance of informality to enhance communication

7. Explicit belief in and recognition of the importance of economic growth and profits[4]

Peters and Waterman particularly emphasize the notions of "being the best," the nuts and bolts of doing the job well, economic growth, and profits. While the content of these values and beliefs varies from company to company and nation to nation, all agree on a more fundamental point: In a world where the rate of change seems to be escalating rapidly, core values provide a source of guidance in the workplace.

Rx for Leaders No. 1   *Warning:* The test of your values is whether they affect your actions in the workplace.

Making Values Explicit

Making corporate values explicit is a significant event in the life of any corporation. But this does not necessarily mean that employees will subscribe to those values, even though they already exist in the corporation in a less structured way. However, defining corporate values or making them explicit does clearly show the corporation's intention to foster those values. An explicit definition of corporate values is often the result of a period of extreme corporate stress, in which the company's survival itself may be in question. Crisis tends to bring a corporation back to fundamentals. Such was the case for Phillips Petroleum.

Phillips Petroleum

Phillips had to fight off two takeover attempts in the 1980s, first by Boone Pickens, then by Carl Icahn. To do so, Phillips had to borrow $5 billion to repurchase stock. Pete Silas, Phillips' CEO, says it was the only

---

[4]Thomas J. Peters and Robert H. Waterman, Jr., *In Search of Excellence,* HarperCollins Publishers, New York, 1982, p. 285, with permission.

way that Phillips could remain an independent company. In addition to having taken on several billion dollars of debt to repurchase stock, Phillips subsequently reduced its workforce by over 25 percent, reduced its assets by about $2 billion, sold all its noncritical businesses, and recaptured excess pension assets. The company that emerged was decidedly different from the old Phillips.

One of the Phillips' planners was particularly interested in the commitment level of Phillips' officers to its corporate mission and objectives. He suspected it was low. He designed and distributed a confidential questionnaire to assess the officers' knowledge of where the corporate mission and objectives came from, whether or not they had participated in defining those objectives, and to what degree they felt a sense of commitment. The answers he received bore out his hunch, indicating that the executives had not participated in drafting the statements, did not know where they came from, and as a result, felt little commitment to them.

Silas's immediate reaction to this information was anger. Upon reflection, though, he conceded: "Well, we better do something about it." At a two-day executive retreat scheduled for the top 25 officers of the corporation, Silas said, in effect, "We are starting over again, from scratch. But this isn't going to be my document. It is going to be ours. That means everyone is going to participate, and everyone is going to own it." The Phillips values and beliefs were a significant product of the meeting:

- Treating one another with respect
- Giving equal opportunity to every employee
- Maintaining a safe work environment
- Conducting ourselves ethically and responsibly
- Communicating openly and honestly
- Supporting individual creativity and innovation
- Providing our customers with top quality and services
- Protecting the environment
- Contributing to the quality of life wherever we operate

The end product does indeed have a high level of ownership.

Rx for Leaders No. 2   Share the definition of your values. There is no better way to secure ownership and commitment than participation

Brunswick

Another turnaround in which focusing more closely on company values played a major role took place at Brunswick in the 1980s. In 1982 Brunswick was forced to sell its medical division to American Home Products to escape a takeover. Brunswick was popularly perceived as having sold its crown jewel to retain its lesser businesses and independent corporate identity.

Over the following five years, however, Brunswick's sales and profits tripled and the return on its equity approached 20 percent, well above historic levels. Jack Reichert, Brunswick's CEO, attributed much of this resurgence to a redefinition of Brunswick's traditional values.

- *Quality:* We will either be the highest-quality producer in every market we serve or we won't be in that business.
- *Customers:* We are in the business to serve customers at a profit. Singularly, customer satisfaction is the most important responsibility we have to assure the long-term success of the company.
- *People:* Of paramount importance is our people—their personal dignity, their pride in what they do, and the trust they have in their management.

Here, in Reichert's own words, are his views on how important the focus on core values was to Brunswick's revival: "Overlying all...was a re-emphasis of the traditional values on which Brunswick had been built. Simply stated, I believe values drive companies...create wealth—but the inverse is not true."[5]

Rx for Leaders No. 3   Talk values as much as you talk numbers. Remember, everyone understands values but not everyone understands numbers.

Herman Miller, Inc.

While some corporations have defined their values more explicitly in a period of external stress, others have done it more proactively to express their distinctiveness.

Herman Miller, Inc. is a leader in participative management. People have specific jobs, but the level of participation on teams and task forces

[5]Jack F. Reichert, "Strategies for an Uncertain Future," speech to the Planning Forum Annual Convention, April 1987, pp. 1–2.

is unparalleled. Herman Miller has a clearly defined set of corporate values:

- *Innovation:* We seek and encourage appropriate problem-solving designs and innovative solutions that deliver results for our customers and meet our business challenges.
- *Excellence:* We create value for our customers by providing quality and excellence in all that we do and the way in which we do it.
- *Participation:* We work together in teams, with each person contributing to the level of his or her capabilities.
- *Ownership:* We each have a stake in the organization in which we invest our lives and share the risks and rewards of ownership.
- *Leadership:* We can lead best by enabling others and by being dedicated to achieving our corporate vision.[6]

Herman Miller likes to sum up the company's values this way: "Innovation and Excellence through Participative Ownership and Leadership." Though Herman Miller is described by some as a maverick company, CEO Max Depree, also a leading business author, thinks that Miller's participative ownership provides a competitive edge and that its strong commitment to shared values is a clear incentive to superior performance.

Cooper Tires

Here's one final example to show that "explicit" need not come at the expense of simplicity. One of the most succinct value statements is the Cooper Tires credo:

Good merchandise, fair play and a square deal.

With only 2.5 percent of the replacement tire market, Cooper consistently achieves a return on its equity approaching 20 percent, nearly twice the industry average. Their approach is simple, uncomplicated, and it works.

Rx for Leaders No. 4   Make your values explicit and succinct. Your people can remember them easily and transform them into action more readily.

---

[6]"Innovation and Excellence through Participative Ownership," A statement of the Herman Miller, Inc., Corporate Values, *Corporate Values,* 1989, with permission.

How Values Relate to Profits

These statements of corporate values raise the important question of how values relate to profits. It is critically important to see values and profits in their proper perspective, as partners and not opponents. *Profit* is viewed with disdain by many who fail to understand its role in the economy at large and as a reward to the superior performer (and its absence as a punishment to those who don't perform). The inclination to disparage the profit motive seems to originate from the medieval concept that one person's profit must always entail another person's loss.

Values are the primary drivers or motivators and profit the reward. Values play the primary motivating role in not-for-profit organizations as well. Here profit translates loosely into the careful stewardship of resources. Just as investment funds pursue the highly profitable performer in the commercial marketplace, charitable giving pursues the good steward with well-communicated values.

Rx for Leaders No. 5   Make values and profits work together toward business success. Neither one can get it done alone.

A Case Study: The Development of IBM's Vision and Values

One of the most prominent examples of vision development in U.S. business history is provided by IBM's early leader, Tom Watson, Sr. IBM was not always a global, multibillion-dollar company. In 1914, at the beginning of World War I, it was just part of a tiny conglomerate that also made scales, time clocks, and related products. Watson came from the National Cash Register Company (NCR) to IBM's predecessor, the Computing-Tabulating-Recording Company (CTR), which then had annual sales of $2.2 million. For the next 42 years, Tom Watson *was* IBM.

Watson was a man of grandiose vision and was dedicated to well-defined and fundamental values. IBM's corporate values, probably the oldest and the best known in the world, were developed by him in the very early days. They are:

- *Respect for the individual:* Respect for the dignity and the rights of each person in the organization.
- *Customer Service:* To give the best customer service of any company in the world.

- *Excellence:* The conviction that an organization should pursue all tasks with the objective of accomplishing them in a superior way.

These short and simple values were the foundation of the IBM vision. Both Tom Watson, Sr., and his successor, Tom Watson, Jr., attribute a great deal of the corporation's success to these fundamental values. Over time, they were converted into broad principles and policies. Finally, they were converted into specific written practices that managers were expected to abide by.

In Tom Watson, Jr.'s recent book, *Father, Son & Co.*, he discusses a letter from his father intended to inspire him to graduate from college: "...always remember life is not as complex as many people would have you think. And the older you grow, the more you will realize that success and happiness depend on a very few things. I list the important assets and liabilities as follows (here he drew a line down the middle of the page and wrote in two columns):

Liabilities	Assets
Reactionary ideas	*Vision*
Love of money!	Unselfishness
Unwholesome companions!	Love
Lax character!	Character (good)
Lack of love for others	Good manners
False friends	Friendship (real)
	Pride in record[7]

Under assets, in addition to vision, Watson, Sr. lists several values: love, good character, good manners, friendship, and unselfishness. The last item listed, Pride in record, is indicative of Watson's belief that vision and values are barren without performance, a subject to be addressed in more detail later in this chapter.

IBM's values have not changed. Despite the company's problems in recent years, its values remain intact. Chapter 14 will examine how well IBM has sustained its corporate values over time.

Rx for Leaders No. 6   Change your values slowly, if at all. They should be a source of stability in a rapidly changing world.

---

[7]Thomas J. Watson, Jr., *Father, Son & Co., My Life at IBM and Beyond*, Bantam Books, New York, 1990, pp. 50–51, with permission.

The IBM Mission

In his college years, Tom Watson, Jr., was a bit skeptical of his father's emphasis on values. He was also skeptical of his father's sense of global mission.

> Father came home from work, gave Mother a hug, and proudly announced that the Computing-Tabulating-Recording Company henceforth would be known by the grand name International Business Machines. I stood in the doorway of the living room thinking, "*That* little outfit?"[8]

The year was 1924. The name was indeed a part of Watson Sr.'s global vision. Its grandeur far exceeded IBM's actual size or influence at that time.

Another critical part of IBM's global vision was a sense of mission. It too was global from the earliest days. In the opening page of his book, Watson, Jr., says of his father, "He had always predicted it would someday be the biggest business on earth."[9] And later he says that his father nurtured sales operations all over the world with the vision that IBM would someday be a very large company. In the author's time at IBM he never saw a corporate mission statement (and it's never been made public to date), but he knew what the mission was: *To be the biggest and most respected company in the world.*

About the time the computer was being introduced to the business world, IBM divested itself of the other businesses (scales and time clocks) that had continued in existence since the early CTR days. The focus of its mission was sharpened and has not been significantly altered since that time. This single-mindedness and sharpness of vision cannot be said to be true of the company that beat IBM to the marketplace with the first computer, Remington Rand. As Tom Watson, Jr., says:

> If Remington Rand had put their money and hearts behind the UNI-VAC right at the start, maybe they'd have been in *Time* magazine instead of us. But nobody at the top of the company had a vision of what computers might mean. Jim Rand was more of a conglomerateur. While Dad was saying, "Shoemaker, stick to your last," Rand's company was selling everything including office equipment, electric shavers, autopilots, and farm machines.[10]

Most other early competitors of IBM also suffered from "split" vision. It cost them dearly.

[8]Ibid, p. 28.

[9]Ibid, p. vii.

[10]Ibid, p. 241.

IBM's desire to be the most respected company in the world led to an undying pursuit of respect and excellence in performance. It also led to a less desirable by-product—fear of failure. As Watson, Jr., himself has said:

> Fear of failure became the most powerful force in my life. I think anybody who gets a job like mine, unless he's stupid, must be a little bit afraid. There is such a long way to fall.[11]

Performance has its price. There was no question about the fear syndrome during those years. Tom Watson, Jr., not only felt it, he created it in others. There was a feeling of family at IBM, and there was a feeling of exhilaration in being with an outstanding and highly respected company. But fear of failure was always an integral part of the corporate culture, and I am certain it remains today.

The IBM Goals

Frank Cary and John Opel, successors to Watson as IBM CEOs, contributed the third part of the IBM vision, the long-term goals to ensure and sustain performance. These goals remain the same today:

- To be the leader in products and services excelling in quality and innovation
- To grow with the industry
- To be the most efficient in everything we do
- To sustain our profitability which funds our growth

For such a huge company, IBM's goals are elegant in their simplicity. The somewhat curious thing to note about IBM goals is that the customer is not mentioned once. When John Akers became CEO in 1985, he corrected that deficiency by adding another goal: To enhance our customer relationships.

The way corporate vision and values are defined is important. In the early 1900s, it was acceptable for Tom Watson, Sr., to define IBM's values personally. Today it is not. Defining values is a shared task of the leader and the leadership group defined as broadly as practical.

Rx for Leaders No. 7   Values are meant to stir the heart, not close the mind. Be open to the important values of your people.

---

[11]Ibid, p. 284.

3
Mission
and Goals

Free men must set their own goals. There is
no one to tell them what to do.[1]

JOHN GARDNER

The corporate mission responds to the second question addressed in the vision statement: What are we today? What are our aspirations for the future? Goals answer the question: What is the corporation committed to achieve? They also set the long-term corporate direction. We will begin with "mission."

Mission: What We Aspire To Be

For many years the corporate mission was considered to be the most fundamental element in a corporation's vision. Only recently was it recognized that a corporation's founder or founders bring a set of fundamental values and beliefs to the birth of their enterprise, generally long before a specific mission or set of goals is established. In *Peak Performers*, Charles Garfield states that "In creating workable missions, there are...predictors of success...putting preference before expertise, draw-

[1]*Excellence*, Harper & Row, New York, 1961, p. 161.

25

ing on the past, trusting intuition, having no preconceived limitations, combining profit with contribution, being pulled by values."[2] His "predictors of success" are excellent guideposts for any organization attempting to articulate a distinctive mission.

It is clear that Garfield believes that the establishment of a corporation's values precedes the defining of its mission. Ideally, the founders of a corporation made their shared values explicit at or shortly after the birth of the company. If they did not, it is up to the current leaders of the company to do so based on all their accumulated knowledge of the founders and the company history since its birth.

A corporate mission should be consistent with the shared values of the corporation. Above all, it should stress "the dignity of the individual." Robert H. Waterman, in his work entitled *The Renewal Factor*, gave this advice to corporate leaders: "Continually examine the causes and commitments that engage you, and the ones you ask of your people, to ensure their basic worth, humanity, and integrity."[3]

Any corporate mission should also have a certain stability. Peter Drucker has said that: "Very few definitions of the purpose and mission of a business have anything like a life expectancy of thirty, let alone fifty, years. To be good for ten years is probably all one can normally expect."[4] But I believe that you must try to think 20 to 30 years ahead to reach the 10-year horizon.

Once established, a corporation's mission should seldom change but should always be subject to reevaluation. It is not unusual to change a word or a phrase in an annual review of a corporate mission, but the changes are seldom drastic. On the other hand, there is no quicker way to send a signal to the organization that a major change is required than to make a significant change in its stated mission.

Rx for Leaders No. 1   Establish your values before you start writing your mission statement. Remember that the founders brought a set of values to the birth of the company, long before a specific mission was defined.

---

[2]Charles Garfield, *Peak Performers*, Avon Books, New York, 1986, p. 93.

[3]From *The Renewal Factor* by Robert H. Waterman, Jr. Copyright © 1987 by Robert H. Waterman, Jr. Used by permission of Bantam Books, a division of Bantam Doubleday Dell Publishing Group, Inc.

[4]Peter F. Drucker, *Management: Tasks, Practices, Responsibilities*, Harper & Row, New York, 1974, p. 89, with permission.

The Key Questions Regarding the Extended Mission

Many managers have found the concept of mission to be very broad and difficult to grasp unless it is broken down into these key elements or questions. The extended mission includes the responses to all four of the following points. The core mission addresses only the first point.

- What is our core mission? What are we today? What do we aspire to be? What is our core competence?
- How will we achieve our corporate aspirations as defined in our core mission statement? What is our internal growth strategy by major business segment? What is our "golden goose"?
- How will we define our external growth strategy to achieve our aspirations if our major business segments do not have adequate internal growth potential?
- What is our long-range financial goal?

Each of these questions will be addressed below. The above elements taken together constitute an *extended* mission statement. The extended mission statement, in a single page, should tell anyone inside or outside the organization who are and we are trying to do.

The basic elements of the extended mission statement go well beyond the traditional *core* mission statement. I feel that the separate elements of the extended statement allow, and in fact force, leaders to be more definitive about their vision. It is not enough that leaders develop a compelling vision; they must also demonstrate credibly how that vision can be realized. An example of an extended mission statement is shown in Fig. 3-1.

What Are We? What Do We Aspire to Be?   The core mission, the first and most fundamental element of the extended mission statement, addresses the questions of what we are today and what we aspire to be in the future. In their desire to get on with what they want to be, many companies do not spend adequate time on what they are. Defining *what we are today* allows us to understand more clearly what we need to change or how we need to change to realize our vision. Phillips Petroleum has done this quite succinctly:

> What we are...an integrated petroleum company that explores for, produces and upgrades oil and natural gas into petroleum products and chemicals for our customers.

ABC Corporation
Extended Mission statement

Core Mission

We provide superior quality industrial and commercial bearings and related support services to our customers. We aspire to be the performance leader in our industry and provide a superior return to our shareholders with particular emphasis on a team effort among our people.

Business Segmentation

The mission for each of the existing businesses is summarized below upon anticipated potential to contribute to the above corporation's long-term goal.

■ **Golden Goose:** *General Aviation Market.* Expand its present base to include commercial and military aircraft through the development and enhancement of metal and successor bearings. Enlarge this thrust to include the industrial and commercial transportation market. Develop the business on a national precision marketing basis.

■ *Selected Market Segments of Strength.* Maintain or increase bearing market share. Develop as a national business. Market through the Bearings Division sales organization as well as the Southern Bearings sales organization.

■ *General Industrial Bearings Market.* Define and target selected segments on a regional, geographic territory basis.

■ *GSA—Military Specifications Business.* Develop on a national account marketing basis.

External
Growth
Strategy

Pursue external growth opportunities aggressively:

- In the aviation/transportation and targeted high growth bearing market segments, pursue technology, or proprietary position.

- In the general industrial bearing business areas, acquire and consolidate as appropriate for economy of scale in manufacturing and/or marketing.

- In the international market, seek additional licensing (buy/sell) agreements.

Long-Term
Financial Goal

Our long-term financial goal is to achieve a total return to shareholders which establishes ABC in the upper quartile of our industry and U.S. industry as a whole.

Figure 3-1 ABC Corporation extended mission statement

Phillips placed particular emphasis on the word "integrated." Much of Phillips' strategy and its "golden goose" can be found in that single word. We will return to this concept shortly.

Following its statement of *what we are,* Phillips defined its future aspirations as follows:

> To enhance the value of our shareholders' investment by using the strengths of our people and our integrated operations to provide our customers with products that are high in quality and competitive in price.[5]

Like the successful firms mentioned by Kotter and Heskett in Chapter 1, the Phillips mission places balanced emphasis on three vital constituencies: customers, people, and shareholders.

Browning Ferris Industries (BFI) provides another example of a core mission:

> Our mission is to provide the highest quality waste collection, transportation, processing, disposal and related services to both public and private customers worldwide.
>
> We will carry out our mission efficiently, safely and in an environmentally responsible manner with respect for the role of government in protecting the public interest.

The first paragraph of the BFI core mission succinctly states what it is today. The second paragraph addresses its aspirations and includes a broad statement of strategic intent.

This statement of strategic intent played a significant role in BFI's decision to discontinue its involvement in the hazardous waste business less than a year later. As CEO William Ruckelshaus said in a letter to employees, "We have tried very hard...to improve the relationship between CECOS (The BFI subsidiary principally responsible for hazardous waste) and various regulatory agencies....We've made major investments of time and capital to upgrade facilities, increase environmental staffing, put in a new audit program and emphasize environmental training programs."[6] Ruckelshaus pointed out that the effort had not been wasted and that BFI could have succeeded in solving its regulatory problems if given enough time and resources. But it had not been able to handle the hazardous waste business "efficiently, safely and in an environmentally responsible manner."

The "Big Dream" or "Strategic Intent."   The second part of the core mission addresses what we aspire to be. In *Servant Leadership,* Robert Greenleaf writes of that "overarching purpose, the big dream, the vision-

---

[5]*PhilNews,* Phillips Petroleum Co. Employee Newsletter, November 1988, p. 8.

[6]*The Blue Line,* Browning-Ferris Industries, Newsletter, April 1990, p. 2.

ary concept...something presently out of reach...so stated that it excites the imagination and challenges people to work for something they do not yet know how to do."[7] Greenleaf's statement captures the visionary element of the mission better than any other that I have seen. When "the big dream" is articulated in this way, it grabs the organization and can become the catapult to business success. Verbalizing the big dream is not always attained in the organization's first attempt; it may take two or even three tries. Some organizations, perhaps most, never attain it.

In the May-June, 1989 issue of the *Harvard Business Review,* Gary Hamel and C. K. Prahalad coined a new term—*strategic intent.* It addressed and gave more definition to Greenleaf's earlier comments. Hamel and Prahalad maintain that "strategic intent captures the essence of winning...is stable over time...sets a target that deserves personal effort and commitment...[and] implies a sizeable stretch for an organization."[8]

Rx for Leaders No. 2 Get your people to focus on aspirations for the future. These aspirations can grab the organization and become the catapult to business success.

Core Competence. The question of *core competence,* or what a corporation is particularly skilled in doing, must be examined as part of its core mission. In the May-June 1990 issue of the *Harvard Business Review,* Hamel and Prahalad state that: "The diversified corporation is a large tree. The trunk and major limbs are core products, the smaller branches are business units; the leaves, flowers, and fruit are end products. The root system that provides nourishment, sustenance, and stability is the core competence....Core competencies are the collective learning in the organization, especially how to coordinate diverse production skills and integrate multiple streams of technologies."[9]

The Pratt & Lambert paint company in Buffalo, New York, defined its core competence in the first sentence of its core mission.

Pratt & Lambert develops, manufactures, and markets coatings and adhesives for decorative and functional applications. Our mission is

[7]Robert K. Greenleaf, *Servant Leadership,* Paulist Press, New Jersey, 1979, pp. 15–16, with permission.

[8]Gary Hamel and C. K. Prahalad, "Strategic Intent," *Harvard Business Review,* May–June 1989, pp. 64, 66, 67.

[9]Reprinted by permission of the *Harvard Business Review.* Excerpt from "The Core Competence of the Corporation" by C. K. Prahalad and Gary Harel (May-June 1990), p. 82. Copyright © 1990 by the President and Fellows of Harvard College, all rights reserved.

to be perceived by our customers as the leader in responding to their product and service needs and to achieve a major share of selected target markets.   ✦

At the time Pratt & Lambert put its mission statement together, this quarter-billion-dollar paint company was organized into six strategic business units, each with its own president. The mission statement was built around a core competence, "coatings and adhesives for decorative and functional applications." These capabilities are what makes Pratt & Lambert most effective and competitive in what it does for its customers in its selected markets. Over time, they must be preserved and expanded.

Distinctive Incompetence. As you examine your core mission, also look at existing product lines and businesses that have not been assets to your corporation. Almost every corporation has these areas. They often create little or no profit on their own, remain a part of the corporation through inaction rather than action, and may be candidates for divestiture.

Drucker says "GE's strategic business planning developed in the late sixties is an exception. [It takes a long and deliberate look at businesses in the portfolio that are poor performers.] Its aim is to answer 'What should our business be?' Yet GE's planning does not start out with the question What new things should we go into?' It starts out with 'What existing product lines and businesses should we abandon?' and 'Which ones should we cut back and deemphasize?'"[10] The GE practice deserves widespread imitation.

Some businesses turn out to be outside the core competence of a corporation. Others do not fit strategically with the corporate vision. For still others, external events may alter the markets dramatically and eliminate earlier growth potential. Growth is the fundamental purpose of strategic planning—the secret to the vitality of an organization—and survival is the reward. If growth prospects are diminished, survival may be in jeopardy. Therefore, these businesses must be divested or spun off before someone else recognizes your weakness, buys your company, and does it for you.

How Will We Achieve Our Corporate Aspirations? *The "Golden Goose."* The definition of the internal corporate growth strategy to achieve our aspirations is critical to an extended mission statement. So is the definition or recognition of the corporate golden goose. All businesses in a corporation are not created equal. There is generally one business that is most

---

[10]Drucker, *Management*, p. 94.

dominant and most profitable. This dominant business is called the "golden goose."

For example, Coca-Cola is in the bottling, movie, and fruit juice businesses. In the past ten years, it has also been in and out of the coffee and wine businesses. However, there is no doubt as to what Coca-Cola's golden goose is. There is a very pithy saying to remind everyone of its importance: Remember the golden goose; feed the golden goose; protect the golden goose at all costs. Coca-Cola got into those other businesses from cash flow provided by its golden goose, and if it were necessary to divest those other businesses in order to protect its golden goose, it would get out of them.

The concept of the golden goose often captures the imagination more than the concept of strategic intent, perhaps because the latter term is more vague or elusive. But not all golden geese are as tangible as that of Coca-Cola. For example, Phillips Petroleum defined its golden goose as the "integrated" nature of the company. In other words, each of its four basic functions (exploration, production, refining, and marketing) is part of an overall dominant business (oil) that Phillips intends to sustain. Phillips' operating unit business strategies are all part of its golden goose, and Phillips has no intention of changing its successful strategies.

In his comment to BFI employees on BFI's discontinuing its involvement in the hazardous waste business, Bill Ruckelshaus pointed out, "The time has come...to shift those human and capital resources to our core business, and pursue the exciting opportunities that we see today in the solid waste area."[11] Solid waste is BFI's golden goose and it will remain so. If Ruckelshaus has his way, recycling solid waste will be BFI's future. There is nothing wrong with golden geese, if you are lucky enough to truly have two of them. Few companies are.

Business Segmentation and Strategy.   The definition of a golden goose is the first step of business segmentation. Companies must also identify their other major business segments, the basic businesses in which the corporation is engaged. There should not be more than a few basic segments, except in a highly diversified corporation. Of course, each segment might be further subdivided at the operating unit level.

Segmenting a corporate business portfolio and defining a strategy for each segment shows how a mission is carried out and its aspirations achieved. If the current organization structure reflects a corporation's future strategy, its segmentation may reflect its basic structure. If not, that may suggest that the basic organizational structure needs revision.

---

[11]*The Blue Line,* p. 2.

Organizational structure should follow strategy, not the reverse. Put another way, organization is the highest level of strategy implementation.

One of the key tasks of creating the extended mission statement is to develop a one-sentence, easily understood statement of the core strategy for each segment. Once this core strategy has been defined or sharpened, you will most likely want to keep it confidential outside the company, since it will become the heart of your competitive strategy. A generalized example of business segmentation and the golden goose is shown in Fig. 3-1.

Rx for Leaders No. 3   Identify your golden goose. Then feed it and protect it at all costs.

What Is Our External Growth Strategy?   Growth opportunities must first be sought and exhausted in your traditional businesses and markets. These should be your areas of distinctive competence and proven performance. There are always industries, however, where there is limited growth or perhaps even negative growth. When growth opportunities begin to diminish for the whole business, or for the golden goose, corporations must seek external growth. There are just a few alternatives:

- Acquisition of similar businesses for consolidation and rationalization opportunities in manufacturing, marketing, or development.
- Cooperative arrangements with similar companies through licensing or joint venture arrangements. These often allow the corporation to expand its geographic or product boundaries with the combined strength of the partners.
- Diversification into unrelated areas (outside the corporation's proven competence).

As a corporation's growth begins to slow, diversification (the last of the alternatives) is often the most coveted and most dangerous. In the early 1980s, when Outboard Marine Corporation (OMC) was anticipating the Japanese invasion of its U.S. market for outboard engines, diversification was a very tempting alternative. Most of OMC's officers had tentatively and reluctantly accepted it as the only way out. However, Charlie Strang, OMC's president and CEO at that time, was adamantly opposed to diversification. His argument was that if the company could not achieve growth and profitability in the only business they really knew, what made them think they could achieve those goals in businesses they knew nothing about? He then steered the OMC battle wagon directly into the oncoming Japanese, and his resolute determination prevented the Japanese from ever gaining more than a 10 percent market share in the United States. The Japanese share is now receding as the ten-year battle continues. OMC holds a 45 percent market share nationwide and roughly a 35 percent share worldwide. Outboards have remained one of the few markets that the Japanese have targeted unsuccessfully.

A critical task in incorporating external growth into an extended mission statement is to examine the long-term growth potential in your traditional markets, match that potential against your growth aspirations, and determine what must be done strategically to address the difference. Not every corporation will include external growth in its final mission statement. For some, traditional markets offer adequate growth opportunities. For others, external growth is an essential part of long-term prospects, and growth goals are usually highly confidential.

A generalized example of an external growth statement is shown in Fig. 3-1. The aviation-transportation business is the ABC Corporation's golden goose, its dominant high-growth business. Here, it seeks a technological and proprietary position in its acquisition strategy. The general industrial bearing market is a commodity business, where the acquisition strategy is based on consolidation to achieve economy of scale in manufacturing, marketing, and so forth. In the international area where the firm is not particularly strong, it would seek partnering arrangements through licensing and joint ventures. The strategy completely avoids diversification although the industry growth rate is slow to slightly negative. The risk of diversification was perceived as being too great while any other alternative remained.

Rx for Leaders No. 4   Search for external growth if the golden goose is aging and has limited growth opportunities. Some companies have maintained consistent double-digit growth in declining industries.

What Is Our Long-Term Financial Goal?   Most CEOs want to see their responsibility to the shareholder reflected high in the priorities of the organization. In most vision statements developed in recent years by publicly held corporations, total return to the shareholder (dividend plus stock price appreciation) is seen as the primary financial goal. Total return is particularly important in those companies that have suffered a recent assault by corporate raiders such as Pickens or Icahn. CEOs generally have little difficulty in defining their financial goal (even if they would not define it precisely as total return to the shareholder) and readily agree that it is a fundamental element of their extended mission statement.

Mission Boundaries

An extended mission statement also establishes boundaries. It sets forth what is *not* intended. In *The Change Masters*, Rosabeth Moss Kanter states that "*leadership* consists in part of keeping everyone's mind on the shared vision, being explicit about `fixed' areas not up for discussion and the constraints on decisions, watching for uneven participation or group pressure, and keeping time bounded and managed."[12] While "management by wandering around" is hailed as a good people strategy, it definitely is not a good vision strategy. The vision must be strong enough to grab and pull the followers along the selected course.

An extended mission statement should never take more than a page. The definition of the golden goose or strategic intent or core competence that grabs its authors, and later (we hope) its followers, may be no more than a phrase or a sentence. The other elements ensure that all the critical strategic questions have been explored explicitly.

The core mission and long-range financial goal are essential elements for the extended mission statement of any corporation. Questions about core competence, the golden goose, and business segmentation must be asked by every corporation but may not apply universally, and the ultimate responses given by the corporation may be unique in character and format. Exploring an extended mission and its elements are intended to prod the corporation to think deeply about itself, not put it in a straitjacket.

Rx for Leaders No. 5   Put some boundaries on your competence through your mission statement. Use it to keep your people's energies and time focused on your company's key strengths.

U.S. Role Models

There is a continuing tendency in the United States to focus on Japanese success stories and underplay our own, especially when examining mod-

---

[12]Rosabeth Moss Kanter, *The Change Masters*, Simon & Schuster, New York, 1983, p. 275.

els of strategic intent or sustained growth. The article by Hamel and Prahalad on strategic intent cited earlier highlights of several Japanese companies who made substantial inroads on the market shares of their American competitors. But it is not necessary to go abroad to make a case for sustained long-term growth. Caterpillar and Xerox are good illustrations of the importance of long-term strategic intent at an earlier period in their corporate lives. IBM, Hewlett Packard, Apple, and Compaq all have illustrated long-term strategic intent in the computer industry.

Over 25 U.S. companies with sales of between $500 million and $5 billion produced compound annual sales growth of above 30 percent in the last half of the 1980s. These included high-tech or high-profile companies like Sun Microsystems (114 percent), Reebok (94 percent), and Compaq (54 percent). Three of the companies are in the somewhat more pedestrian auto parts and products industry. They include Mark IV Industries (84 percent), Sudbury (66 percent), and Harvard Industries (60 percent). Costco Wholesale (97 percent) and Price (34 percent) are warehouse clubs. More traditional companies include Maytag (37 percent), BASF (36 percent), and Morgan Stanley (34 percent). Conner Peripherals, with 1991 sales of over $1 billion, did not make the list because it was not in business until 1987. Finally, in most industries, the profit margins of U.S. companies are higher than those of their Japanese counterparts. We do not need Japanese role models.

Rx for Leaders No. 6   Look to U.S. companies for role models. Your people will have an easier time identifying with Reebok or Bank One or Dell. The Japanese did not invent superior business performance.

Goals: What We Are Committed to Achieve

The third element of the corporate vision is the statement of long-term goals. Goals answer the question, "What is the corporation committed to achieve?" and set the long-term corporate direction. They identify what we want to accomplish and provide directional guidance for conducting business. Like corporate values and mission, goals take the long view with little change anticipated over the short term. Goals should expand on and flow out of mission and values. The corporation must also be able to translate them into specific strategies and tactics, which we will discuss in Chap. 4.

Drucker states that the purpose and mission of a business have to be translated into goals. If not, they become merely good intentions which may never be achieved. He also states that goals:

- Must be derived from what our business is
- Are not abstractions
- Must be capable of being converted into specific targets and specific assignments
- Must make possible *concentration* of resources and efforts
- Must be multiple rather than single....To manage a business is to balance a variety of needs and goals
- Are needed in all areas on which the *survival* of the business depends.[13]

Participation in Goal Setting Ensures Commitment

There are several critical characteristics involved in effective goal setting:

- Participation
- Freedom
- Ownership
- Commitment

It is the leaders of a corporation who must set goals, and they must be given maximum freedom is doing so. That gives them ownership of and ultimately commitment to the goals. They must also be given the right to help establish their supporting goals for their own function or business unit.

Several other elements are critical to the proper formation and shaping of effective goals:

- Focus
- Challenge
- Breadth
- Priority

Too many goals can make a corporate effort overly fragmented, or at least appear that way. The focus achieved by having not more than

[13]Drucker, *Management,* pp. 99–100.

three to five corporate goals can be very effective in its simplicity. Everyone can more readily commit the goals to memory, which will make them more likely to internalize and, ultimately, implement the goals. Goal statements themselves should be limited to perhaps ten words or fewer, since the objective is clarity and simplicity instead of vagueness and complexity.

Goals must also mirror the parent mission statement in terms of their aspirations. In this sense, they must contain challenge and inspire everyone to their best efforts. While they should be clear and to the point, goals must also be stated in sufficient breadth that they need not be changed or modified every year or two. That generally means that no numbers should be included. Quantifications will come later with very specific accountability (see Chap. 4). Finally, the leader who establishes the goals must be prepared for the inevitable question of goal priority, which I will address shortly.

Rx for Leaders No. 7   Share the goal-setting responsibility with your leadership team. Give them the freedom to help you set challenging corporate goals and their own supporting goals.

Simple Goals Are Effective Goals

IBM makes the case for a limited number of goals very effectively. With over 300,000 employees operating in over 100 nations around the world, IBM has had the same four corporate goals for many years:

- To be the leader in products and services excelling in quality and innovation
- To grow with the industry
- To be the most efficient in everything we do
- To sustain our profitability which funds our growth

Distilling the corporate mission of a worldwide organization such as IBM into only four goals is elegant in its simplicity. It certainly impressed Fred Stratton, the CEO of Briggs & Stratton, on a visit to IBM corporate headquarters that included discussions with six or seven IBM executives. The first speaker of the day asked Stratton whether he was aware of IBM's corporate goals. Stratton indicated that he was not. The speaker then outlined the four goals and related what his department or function accomplished in relation to the goals. Stratton was impressed.

He was even more impressed when the next speaker did exactly the same thing. But he was amazed when all the speakers related their job or function to the basic IBM goals and stated what role they played in achieving them. It was obvious that the simplicity and focus of the IBM corporate goals allowed their ownership to extend far beyond the corporate leadership group and dig deeply into the organization.

None of the IBM goals contain a fixed quantitative target. This should not be surprising if we remember that the purpose of a goal is to set direction for the long term. In setting broader, directional goals, we retain the flexibility to change tactical targets from year to year, depending on circumstances. Setting these tactical targets would be affected by the following factors: Is the industry in a period of growth, consolidation, or is its very survival in question? Is the economy expanding rapidly, growing slowly, or moving erratically? What is happening to inflation rates, currency exchange rates, and the intensity of global competition? In the goal-setting phase, one must be concerned with direction, motivation, and critical relationships, not hard numbers.

Rx for Leaders No. 8   Focus your vision. Keep the number of goals limited, but make them broad enough to stand the test of time.

The Priority of Goals

The priority of goals still needs to be addressed. If the leaders do not establish a system of priority for their goals, their people will. In IBM's goals, there is a definite system of priority, or at the very least a consistent order. Products and services excelling in quality and innovation is goal number one. It is also clear that goal number four, profitability, ties the other goals together, and at the same time is a measure of success. Between the other two goals, growth (goal number two) probably weighs somewhat more on the IBM mind than productivity (goal number three). Another rationale for the sequence is that leadership in products and services will bring the growth. Growth, combined with efficiency in everything IBM does will bring the profit. And the profit in turn fuels additional growth. As mentioned in Chap. 2, when John Akers became CEO of IBM many years after these goals were first established, he added a new goal, "To enhance customer relationships" and made it number one.

Goals do not always have to be prioritized. Some companies might say their goals are equal or balanced in importance. But the goals should be sequenced in such a way that an effective rationale can be constructed as they are presented to the various constituencies. People can then readily understand the goals and commit to their interrelationship.

Browning-Ferris Industries also has a carefully selected order for their five corporate goals:

Quality: Provide the highest quality service to our customers to guarantee their satisfaction.

Growth: Assure long-term growth and increase market share.

People: Ensure that BFI has the people necessary to carry out our mission.

Ethical conduct: Manage our business in a manner consistent with the public interest.

Financial: Achieve consistently superior results that maintain BFI as a premier growth organization and maximize shareholder value.

Like IBM, BFI made quality goal number one, and also emphasized the ultimate measure of quality, customer satisfaction. Note the one- or two-word handle on each goal that makes it even easier to grasp and remember. BFI's number two goal is growth, but it is even more strongly stated than IBM's, with special emphasis placed on increasing market share. As a service business, BFI is particularly dependent on its employees, and thus, its number three goal emphasizes the importance of people. Its number four goal addresses ethical conduct, which is also emphasized both in the company's mission and in its values. The financial goal emphasizes BFI's commitment to be "a premier growth organization and maximize shareholder value."

It was questions regarding the last two goals, ethical conduct and financial performance, that led BFI to discontinue its hazardous waste business less than a year after the plan was completed. A clear set of goals can help a corporation's leaders decide whether to enter or exit a business.

Rx for Leaders No. 9   Decide on a rational sequence for your goals. Ask yourself the question of goal priority, or your people will.

The Nobility of the Cause

An important aspect of goals is the leader and leadership team's perception of their inherent importance. "A final place to look for trouble is in the inherent nobility—or ignobility—of the cause. If the focus is only on cost reduction, the atmosphere that surrounds it is usually dour. If the focus is on quality, service, or revenue enhancement, the process has an inherently positive spirit."[14]

Two of the most frequently occurring and fundamentally important corporate goals or "causes" are *growth* and *return to the shareholder*. Most U.S. executives worship openly and frequently at both altars. Alfred P. Sloan, Jr.'s credo for General Motors was succinct: "Growth is essential to the good health of an enterprise. Deliberately to stop growing is to suffocate." Growth is the most fundamental indicator of corporate health and probable survival.

Many mature companies that have trouble with growth blame their problems on their age or the age of their industry, with the implication that growth belongs to the start-up and younger companies. But this is not so. The Cognetics Growth Index finds that companies over 75 years old have a higher growth rate, 10.4 percent, than younger companies. The next highest growth rate, 7.4 percent, is found among companies 50 to 74 years old, followed by the start-ups (0 to 4 years old) at 6.8 percent. Growth remains a fundamental corporate goal in all stages of corporate life.

With regard to *return to the shareholder,* it would seem that performance pays off and is a goal worth striving for. "The ten stocks on *Fortune's* 1989 list of the Most Admired corporations were up collectively about 40 percent last year, not including dividends. The complete list is as follows:[15]

Philip Morris	63.4%	Shell Oil	N/A
PepsiCo	62.0%	Merck	34.2%
Boeing	47.0%	3M	28.4%
Rubbermaid	46.3%	Exxon	13.6%
Wal-Mart	43.0%	Herman Miller	−.6%

Goals Complete the Corporate Vision Statement

A hypothetical corporate vision statement (values, mission, and goals) is shown schematically in Fig. 3-2. The fundamental values are shown on top permeating the mission and the goals. Only the core mission statement is shown.

[14]Robert H. Waterman, Jr., *The Renewal Factor,* p. 261.
[15]Bruce W. Jolesch, *Fortune.* February 12, 1990, p. 38, with permission.

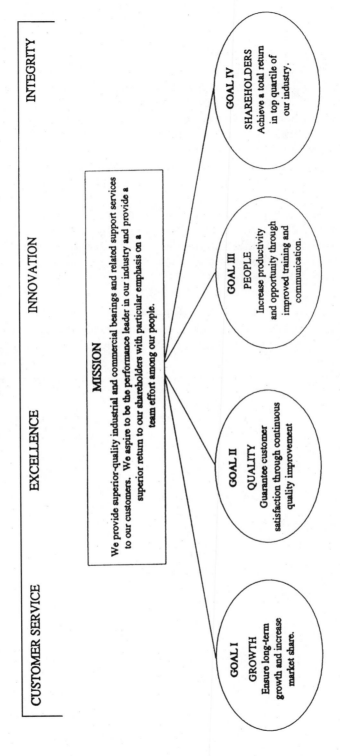

Figure 3-2 ABC Corporation—Vision Statement and Slogan (schematic).

The vision statement is not a closed-end proposition. It may also contain a slogan, a diagram, a picture—whatever grabs your attention. The aim of the slogan or battle cry at the bottom of Fig. 3-2 is to capture the essence of the more formal parts of the vision in a few words that are easily remembered yet evoke the spirit of the entire vision statement. For Canon in its 20-year-plus battle with Xerox, the slogan or battle cry was "Beat Xerox." Toyota's is just as brief, but broader-based: "To Win." Motorola's slogan is "Total Customer Satisfaction." Outboard Marine Corporation's slogan is "To Take the World Boating." Chevron strives "To Become Better than the Best."

Corporate goals perform one other vital function. They provide linkage with the yet-to-be-developed strategic plans, operating plans, financial plans, etc. Goals link the desired world expressed in the values and mission with the company's actual strategies and tactics to realize their vision in the real world.

Rx for Leaders No. 10   Link your vision statement with your strategies and tactics through a set of goals that are both focused and challenging.

4

Strategies and Tactics

Ensuring Commitment and Accountability

Even the most compelling leadership vision will fail without sound strategies and tactics to make the vision a reality. While the primary thrust of this book is the leaders' vision and values, this chapter is dedicated to the necessary strategies, tactics, and accountability statements that comprise the supporting strategic business plan.

"Going from formulating vision to implementing it [is] more like proceeding gradually along a continuum than crossing over a bridge...to unrelated territory. To the left of the continuum is the intuitive, future vision of the organization, which is in the heads and hearts of the top management team."[1] Strategies and tactics might be pictured near the center of the continuum. They grow out of the vision statement, but they guide or direct the day-to-day operations and decision making. To the right are operating plans and budgets that translate vision into action. From the left to the right of the continuum strategic thinking evolves gradually into operations.

Strategies and tactics are statements of the organization's commitment to implementing its goals. Tactics, in particular, establish the basis for accountability. They allow the organization to measure its progress in achieving its vision in a timely manner.

[1]Benjamin B. Trego, John W. Zimmerman, Ronald A. Smith, and Peter M. Tobia, *Vision in Action: Putting a Winning Strategy to Work,* Simon & Schuster, New York, 1989, p. 33. Copyright © 1989 by Kepner Tregoe, Inc., with permission.

The leader must be personally involved to ensure linkage of the vision to the supporting strategic plan.

Rx for Leaders No. 1   Develop sound strategies and tactics, or even the most compelling leadership vision will fail. Leaders must ensure that the selected strategies and tactics move the corporation toward its vision in a timely manner.

Commitment Requires Trust

Implementation of a vision depends on commitment to goals. And commitment depends on trust in the leader or leaders of the organization. "Trust is the lubrication that makes it possible for organizations to work....The truth is that we trust people who are predictable, whose positions are known and who keep at it; leaders who are trusted make themselves known, make their positions clear."[2]

This trust will not be blind trust for those whom the leader involves in the formulation of the corporate vision. They will trust not just their leader but their group as a whole and themselves individually. Strategies, tactics, and accountability statements commit the leader and the group in terms of what they intend to do in the near-term future to achieve their ultimate vision. Strategies and tactics imply consistency, constancy, and a willingness to be evaluated on the results.

Rx for Leaders No. 2   Demonstrate consistency in your strategy and tactics and a willingness to be measured on results. Leaders must be predictable.

Strategic Planning: A Fundamental Leadership Process

This chapter will address strategic planning in order to demonstrate its relationship to the corporate vision and the day-to-day planning and

---

[2]Warren Bennis and Burt Nanus, *Leaders: The Strategies for Taking Charge,* Harper Collins Publishers, Inc., New York, 1985, pp. 43–44. Copyright © 1985 by Warren Bennis and Burt Nanus.

decision making that flow from it. Part IV of the text, "Linking Vision and Values to Strategic Planning," examines other aspects of the relationship of the corporate vision and values to strategic planning.

Figure 4-1 shows the three principal elements of the corporate vision and of the strategic plan. It also highlights the strategic question that each element addresses. It emphasizes the long-range time horizon of the corporate vision and the medium- to short-range time horizon of the strategic plan. While a corporate vision statement is seldom revised, and then only for clarification, a strategic plan will need to be modified annually. As we have stated, quantitative content does not exist in a corporate vision, while the quantitative content of a strategic plan is quite high for purposes of both measurement and accountability.

A corporate vision statement cannot achieve its desired impact unless it is communicated broadly. It should not be seen as a confidential document, but rather, it is intended to convey to employees, customers, shareholders, and vendors the nature of the company and its aspirations. Generally, this is not true of a strategic plan. There may be some parts of it that can be made public. But there are also parts of almost any organization's strategic plan that are not public, particularly if it is a for-profit organization that is in any type of direct competition. For this reason, it is almost impossible to use real-life illustrations of strategies and tactics.

Strategies

Strategies answer the questions: How do we achieve our long-term goals? How are we going to make those goals a reality? How are we going to get there? As goals grow out of the mission statement, so do strategies grow out of long-term goals. Furthermore, each strategy should generate and be supported by a number of tactics or action plans and programs. Strategies have a relatively long life but are subject to annual evaluation. They are primarily qualitative in nature, so they must be converted into tactics and quantified accountability statements.

In general, firms should develop three to five meaningful strategies per goal, listed in some rational or priority order. For ease of communication and understanding, they should begin with verbs and be kept to no more than one sentence.

Figure 4-2 shows a typical set of strategies for the fictitious ABC Corporation. The ABC Corporation's "people" goal (goal for its employees) is to "increase productivity and opportunity through improved training and communication." The three broad strategies in support of the people goal address productivity and training to enhance opportunity, as well as communications and loyalty. The management of ABC saw the three strategies as sufficiently broad to cover just about anything they might

Corporate Vision

	Strategic Question	Horizon	Revision	Quantitative Content
Shared values	What do we stand for?	Long	Seldom, for clarification	None
Mission	Why do we exist?	Long	Seldom, for clarification only	None
Goals	What are we committed to do?	Long	Seldom, for clarification only	None

Strategic Plan

	Strategic Question	Horizon	Revision	Quantitative content
Strategies	How do we achieve our long-term goals?	Medium	Annually, if necessary	Very little
Tactics	What short-term programs are needed?	Short-Medium	Annually, as necessary	High
Accountability	How will we measure progress? Who has primary responsibility? When must the programs be completed?	Short-Medium	Annually, as necessary	High

Figure 4-1. Corporate vision and strategic plan.

```
┌─────────────────────────────────────────────────────────────┐
│              ABC Corporation Sample Strategies              │
│                                                             │
│  GOAL 3:   PEOPLE   Increase productivity and opportunity through │
│                     improved training and communication.    │
│       Strategy 3.1  Improve participation and productivity. │
│       Strategy 3.2  Provide training to enhance opportunity. │
│       Strategy 3.3  Improve communications and strengthen   │
│                     loyalty.                                │
└─────────────────────────────────────────────────────────────┘
```

Figure 4-2.

want to do on a tactical basis regarding communicating with their people and providing for their growth. The test of the breadth of the strategies will come in the next step, when the firm must define tactically and specifically what it will do, when it will do it, and who will get it done.

Figure 4-3 shows a sample set of strategies for the XYZ Photocopier Machine Company. XYZ has outlined the four strategies it believes to be critical in achieving its goal to "ensure long-term growth and increase market share." Once again, the final test will be the development of specific tactics supporting these strategies.

Tactics and Accountability

Tactics answer the question: What short-term programs are needed to support a particular strategy? They describe the specific programs supporting the broad strategies and are operational in nature. Tactics are short-range action plans that are subject to continued evaluation and changes in direction and emphasis. A significant number should be

```
┌─────────────────────────────────────────────────────────────┐
│              XYZ Corporation Sample Strategies              │
│                                                             │
│  GOAL 1:   Ensure long-term growth and increase market share. │
│    Strategy 1.1   Develop and maintain aggressive market strategies │
│                   for each business segment.                │
│    Strategy 1.2   Continue development of formal product plans │
│                   and forecasts for each product/market/business │
│                   segment.                                  │
│    Strategy 1.3   Extend the personal copier product lines. │
│    Strategy 1.4   Develop and maintain overall marketing policies │
│                   and guidelines.                           │
└─────────────────────────────────────────────────────────────┘
```

Figure 4-3.

completed in the 12 months following completion of the strategic plan. The completed tactics must be replaced by new action plans addressing another aspect of the strategy.

The best tactics are output-oriented; that is, they emphasize what the corporation hopes to get out of the action plan. For example, when what you really need is to "realize a 20 percent sales increase," state that instead of "hire ten new salespeople." Tactics should be kept brief and begin with "hard" verbs, such as "implement," "establish," or "recommend." These words will make it clear to the observer that you either accomplished something specific or you didn't and that the results can be measured. Minimize the use of "soft" verbs like "define," "study," or "analyze," since the results of these tactics are not readily measurable.

The accountability side of a tactic concerns itself with measurability, responsibility, and timeliness. The best accountability statements will have quantitative, measurable content, such as "increase sales by 10 percent," "achieve a 15 percent ROA." For first-generation plans, this would mean about 50 percent of the tactics or more should be quantified in some way. They will identify a single person by name or office as primarily responsible beyond any joint efforts, committees, and so forth. The person responsible must consider the tactic and accountability statement doable, though it may be ambitious. All accountability statements should include a target completion date. When the completion date is more than one year in the future, include a start date and a status check date or dates.

Rx for Leaders No. 3   Keep your people focused on the economic or organizational benefit desired as a result of a tactic. Without your help in this area your people will tend to focus on the action plan itself (or the investment required).

Figure 4-4 shows a set of sample tactics and accountability statements for the ABC Corporation supporting its strategy to achieve total plan commitment. The tactics address what the ABC Corporation considered to be four basic elements in achieving an effective planning process.

Figure 4-5 demonstrates schematically how strategies and tactics discussed in this chapter fit with the corporate vision discussed in Chapters 1 through 3. The top part of the schematic was shown as Fig. 3-1 in Chap. 3, as we completed the discussion of long-term goals. Figure 4-5 depicts three or four strategies for each of four goals of the ABC Corporation. The bottom part of the page, which treats tactics and accountability, shows one of the supporting tactics for each strategy.

The tactic shown was selected by the developers of the plan as the

---

ABC Corporation—Sample Tactics

STRATEGY 4.4   Achieve total commitment to the strategic planning process.

Tactic 4.4.1   Establish a Corporate Strategic Planning Council to address key corporate issues and guide the overall process. Meet monthly. VP Corporate Planning. Complete: 12/199X.

Tactic 4.4.2   Develop coordinated strategic plan roll-out process. VP Corporate Planning. Complete: 1/199X.

Tactic 4.4.3   Implement strategic control of plan implementation through Strategic Planning Council. Meet quarterly. VP Corporate Planning. Complete: 3/199X, quarterly thereafter.

Tactic 4.4.4   Establish annual plan revision process. VP Corporate Planning. Complete: 12/199X, yearly thereafter.

Figure 4-4.

key, or most important, of the tactics supporting that strategy. From this single page, a board member, employee, or selected outsider can see at a glance how the overall corporate vision and strategic plan complement and support each other. Tactics represent a consistent set of action plans or programs to achieve a desired strategic result. The best tactics are output oriented and describe the desired end result.

Rx for Leaders No. 4   Share the leadership burden. Create an enhanced sense of personal responsibility by assigning tactical responsibility to as many people as possible.

Measurability and Doability

As indicated earlier, each tactic should contain its own basis of measurement. David Packard, the cofounder of Hewlett-Packard, says that people's actions are based on how they are measured.[3] Robert

---

[3]David Packard, *Harvard Business Review*, November-December, 1988, p. 194.

**ABC CORPORATION
SHARED VALUES**

CUSTOMER SERVICE   EXCELLENCE   INNOVATION   INTEGRITY

MISSION

We provide superior quality industrial and commercial bearings and related support services to our customers. We aspire to be the performance leader in our industry and provide a superior return to our shareholders with particular emphasis on a team effort among our people.

GOAL I

GROWTH
Ensure long-term growth and increase market share.

GOAL II

QUALITY
Guarantee customer satisfaction through continuous quality improvement.

GOAL III

PEOPLE
Increase productivity and opportunity through improved training and communication.

GOAL IV

SHAREHOLDERS
Achieve a total return in top quartile of our industry.

STRATEGIES

1.1 Structure sales and marketing organization to better address customer needs.
1.2 Increase sales of products in existing markets.
1.3 Pursue sales of products to new markets.

TACTICS & ACCOUNTABILITY

1.1.1 Install sales/marketing structure which aligns with product lines yet maintains current 10% of G&A expenses: Gen. Mgr. Mktg; B:10/93, S:4/94, C:12/94.
1.2.1 Achieve 90% or more of field sales force reaching 100% of sales targets: Sales Mgr.; B:6/93, S:9/93, C:12/93.
1.3.1 Identify opportunities in aircraft and/or transportation market which are likely to return above our average 3.6% ROS and which represent at least $10 million in new revenues: Mgr. Mkt. Research; B:12/93, S:3/94, C:9/94.

STRATEGIES

2.1 Implement feedback systems to ensure a high level of customer service.
2.2 Realign resources to effectively meet customer needs.
2.3 Provide an effective quality assurance program.

TACTICS & ACCOUNTABILITY

2.1.3 Administrate an effective, annual customer opinion survey, highlighting product improvements to achieve 15–20% response rate: Mgr. Mkt. Research; B:12/93, S:6/94, C:9/95.
2.2.4 Reduce manufacturing/distribution costs by 12% and response/delivery time by 5%: Mgt. Operations; B:12/93; S:6/94; C:9/95.
2.3.1 Implement a new quality control organization structure eliminating 2 layers of management by shifting responsibility for quality to shop floor operators: Mgr. Quality Control: B:12/93, S:9/94, C:3/95.

STRATEGIES

3.1 Improve participation and productivity.
3.2 Provide training to enhance opportunity.
3.3 Improve communications and strengthen loyalty.

TACTICS & ACCOUNTABILITY

3.1.2 Design employee involvement program to address cost and quality issues; achieve voluntary participation goals of: B:7/93
- 40% of emp. participating by 3/94
- 60% of emp. participating by 9/94
Director of Human Resources.
3.2.1 Establish specific training and development programs for all people: B:9/93
- > 80% of hourly employees by 3/94
- > 80% of management by 6/94
Director of Human Resources.
3.3.2 Institute weekly supervisory reports based on brief meetings to encourage employee communication of key concerns: Ops. Mgr.; B:9/93 — 85% supervisory compliance by 9/95.

STRATEGIES

4.1 Achieve financial benchmarks relative to competitors.
4.2 Achieve revenue growth goal at a targeted selling price/unit.
4.3 Achieve total commitment and active participation in planning process.

TACTICS & ACCOUNTABILITY

4.1.2 Attain return on equity of 16% or better (Top quartile of industry): GM; B:6/93, S:Quarterly, C:Yearly.
4.2.2 Achieve CAGR in revenues of 7% or more: GM Mktg. & Sales; B:6/93, S:Quarterly, C:Yearly.
4.4.3 Implement strategic control of plan implementation through quarterly reviews by Strategic Planning Council. Meet quarterly: VP Corp. Planning; C:3/94, quarterly thereafter.

Note:
B: Begin
S: Status Check
C: Complete

Figure 4-5. ABC Corporation—schematic of vision statement and strategic plan. (*Continued*)

Waterman expands on the same concept: "If you're looking for quick ways to change how an organization behaves...change the measurement system, or change even one measure. Conversely, if you can't figure out why things aren't changing, look to the measurement system. Measures are an important part of both the explicit and implicit systems for paying attention."[4] Each tactic should contain its own basis of measurement. It is natural to resist this because measurability makes accountability quite precise. The only way that you will get adequate measurability is to insist on it.

Finally, people must believe that the task assigned to them is doable. "Long-term improvement comes only if the attention employees receive communicates their manager's genuine belief that they can do what is expected of them. Believable, positive expectations yield positive results. Unbelievable or negative expectations beget the opposite."[5]

Rx for Leaders No. 5   Handle the accountability side of each tactic with care. It defines the basis for measurability and is the source of stewardship.

Responsibility

Each tactic statement designates a specific manager as responsible. This should seldom be the CEO. One of the fundamental purposes of the plan is to allow the CEO to share responsibility and enable others to assume it. Even when the CEO is required to make a final decision, the responsibility portion should designate the manager responsible for marshaling the qualitative or quantitative information necessary to make that decision.

> The taking of responsibility is at the heart of leadership. To the extent that leadership tasks are shared, responsibility is shared....For every person now leading, there are many more who could share leadership tasks, testing their skills, enjoying the lift of spirit that comes with assuming responsibility.[6]

---

[4]From *The Renewal Factor* by Robert H. Waterman, Jr. Copyright © 1987 by Robert H. Waterman, Jr. Used by permission of Bantam Books, a division of Bantam Doubleday Dell Publishing Group, Inc.

[5]Ibid, p. 261.

[6]Reprinted with the permission of the Free Press, a division of Macmillan, Inc. from *On Leadership* by John W. Gardner. Copyright © 1990 by John W. Gardner.

Assigning responsibility for each task to somebody other than the CEO not only spreads the leadership burden around, it makes it more manageable. Equally important, it motivates and creates an enhanced sense of personal responsibility for each tactic, which should be clearly designated even if a team effort is required.

Rx for Leaders No. 6   Show your people they can jump a couple of hurdles in terms of accepting responsibility. The next time they will raise the challenge level themselves.

Bottom-up vs. Top-down

The schematic shown in Fig. 4-5 would imply that there is a natural progression from value to mission to goal to strategy to tactics and accountability statements. And logically, there is. But the whole process is iterative in nature. *There must be an effective bottom-up as well as a top-down flow of ideas in any organization. A successful organization will be sensitive to both.*

A leader had better have his or her ear to the ground for messages from the troops on the operational firing line. Breakthrough strategies are as dependent on bottom-up feedback as they are on top-down vision. Nevertheless, the role of the leader in calling for a change in direction is still critical. "Strong leaders articulate direction and save the organization from change via `drift.' They create a vision of a possible future that allows themselves and others to see more clearly the steps to take, *building on present capacities and strengths.*"[7]

Rx for Leaders No. 7   Make certain your planning process accommodates a bottom-up as well as a top-down flow of ideas.

"The Boss's Grand Plan"

Senior management is often given low scores by their people for their visioning efforts on "the grand plan." In a letter to the editor of *The Wall Street Journal,* a middle manager vents some of his frustrations and makes some telling points:

[7]Rosabeth Moss Kanter, *The Change Masters,* Simon & Schuster, New York, 1983, pp. 294–295.

In your Labor Letter column of Feb. 9, I see that executives complain of foot dragging by middle managers who "focus too much on fighting fires and resolving operating issues and not enough time on the boss's grand plan." Before we do too much hand-wringing over top management's plight, let's consider some other points of view....

First, the chief executive officer's brainchild is too often only his or, at best, the result of negotiations among senior executives and consultants whose knowledge of business units begins and ends with "the numbers." More, their products either become top secret or are poorly communicated to the operating level. When a general manager is no more than polite to an executive scheme that he had no hand in building, no one should be surprised.

As to content, let's face it, much "grand" thinking at the top is not. Many otherwise respectable managements permit themselves the delusion that they are providing "vision" when they are merely projecting today's business ahead in time. Sorry, but summing business units' annual plans and pushing them out as far as the spreadsheet will go doesn't make it as valid strategy.[8]

> [Signed] M. R. Eigerman
> Vice President, Strategy Management
> Semcor

This letter is thought-provoking and I believe it represents the feelings of a good number of middle managers, although not many would vent their feelings in public. The letter makes at least two significant points:

- There must be a vision and set of values that are clearly enunciated and communicated.

- There must also be a visible and credible plan for making that vision a reality.

Top management has the primary responsibility for developing a corporate vision and values, and operating management has primary responsibility for developing the strategic or implementation plans. Neither part is of much value if the other part is flawed. The letter to the editor indicates an apparent flaw in top management's ability to *communicate and gain support* for their vision and values. Their lack of communication with their employees has resulted in a low level of *trust*, which brings with it tremendous loss of energy and effectiveness in any organization. The problem is magnified significantly in the global organization, where in many locations leaders are seldom seen or heard.

---

[8]Letters to the Editor, *The Wall Street Journal*, February 26, 1988, p. 15, with permission.

Part III of this book will address communicating and gaining support for the corporate vision and values.

Strategy vs. Analytical Techniques

Over the last 20 years, consulting firms specializing in corporate strategy have developed a myriad of analytical tools and techniques that are frequently confused with strategy itself. The tools include the experience curve, the learning curve, economy of scale derivatives, the portfolio matrix, and so forth. When discussing these or any other planning techniques, there is a critical differentiation that must be made. Making use of planning tools and techniques does not constitute strategy. All these tools are analytical. They provide the foundation or the stepping-off point for strategy. Strategy involves a very high level of *synthesis*, which means putting all the analytical pieces together into a meaningful whole, a broad course of action leading to a desirable goal. That is what strategy is all about.

Many CEOs (as well as the core group of leaders involved in the development of corporate strategy) almost intuitively recognize this difference and ask the same question, "Why this overemphasis on techniques?" Perhaps the answer lies in the basic structure of the consulting firms developing the techniques, the consulting pyramid that forms the underpinning of many consulting firms.

Consulting Pyramid

Daily Rate		Role
$6000	o	Finder
$3000	o o	Binder
$1500	o o o o	Minder
$ 750	o o o o o o o	Grinder

At the base of this pyramid is the recently graduated MBA, the Grinder, who possesses a high degree of intelligence, personal drive, and a mind that can absorb techniques and data at a tremendous rate. The Minders are responsible for directly overseeing the analysis tasks of the Grinders. The Binders are responsible for account management and further business development within client accounts. The Finders are generally at the partner or managing director level. Their daily rate is high, but that is not visible to the client in the consultant's billing, which homogenizes everything into an average hourly rate.

The ratio of one Minder to every two Grinders is essential because of the Grinders' lack of experience. The Grinders are generally one to two years out of business school. Since their compensation is about one-third of their billing rate, they can be paid $40,000–$80,000 a year and still be highly profitable. In fact, they are the real profit generators in the firm, if they are kept under client contract.

In this context, a consulting firm's overemphasis on technique is quite understandable. The young MBA is the key to profitability. While lacking business experience, the MBA can more than handle rote technique, and graduate business school training has put a sharp edge on his or her analytical capabilities. While this has prepared the MBA for analysis and problem definition, he or she is often ill-prepared for the more difficult problems of synthesis and strategy.

That is the job of corporate leaders and the subject of this book, namely, developing a compelling corporate vision, sharing it with others both inside and outside the corporation, and then sustaining that vision over time.

Rx for Leaders No. 8   Keep the distinction between strategy and analysis clear. Young MBAs often do an excellent job of utilizing analytical techniques. But only leaders can set a strategy for the corporation.

PART 2

The Leadership Conference Planning Process: "How to Do It"

- Focuses on vision formation and the underlying Leadership Conference Planning Process (LCPP)—a fifth generation planning process
- Reviews the preparation required for successful conferences as well as the theme and format of each conference

5

Selecting the Core Group

Motorola is well known for its "Six Sigma Quality" program and for winning the Malcolm Baldrige Award. But its quality program is only one part of its overall corporate vision, which is both simple and easily illustrated (see Fig. 5-1, which depicts Motorola's laminated wallet-sized corporate vision card). Motorola's vision statement emphasizes four major business segments and the company's fundamental objective of total customer satisfaction.

Figure 5-2 shows Motorola's key beliefs and three key goals—an admirable focus! "Six Sigma Quality" is the first of five key initiatives or major strategies.

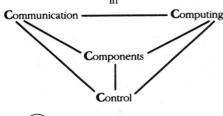

Figure 5-1. Motorola, Inc. fundamental objective.

KEY BELIEFS—*how we will always act*

- Constant Respect for People
- Uncompromising Integrity

KEY GOALS—*what we must accomplish*

- Increased Global Market Share
- Best in Class
  —*People*
  —*Marketing*
  —*Technology*
  —*Product*
  —*Manufacturing*
  —*Service*
- Superior Financial Results

KEY INITIATIVES—*how we will do it*

- Six Sigma Quality
- Total Cycle Time Reduction
- Product and Manufacturing Leadership
- Profit Improvement
- Participative Management Within, and
  Cooperation Between Organizations

Figure 5-2. Motorola, Inc. key beliefs, key goals, and key initiatives.

It looks so simple when it is completed. But if you are still on square one, the natural questions are: "Where did it come from?" and "How do you put it together?"

How To Do It

The purpose of this and the following chapters is to clearly define how vision can be developed and defined. I call the process which I developed to formulate the vision *the leadership conference planning process* (LCPP). The name is derived from *who* is involved in defining a corporate vision, *how* they do their work, and *what* it is they do. First, the process involves the leadership of the organization. Second, the process is based on a series of three conferences. Third, the process is primarily a planning process.

By "how to do it" I mean an explicit description of how the vision can be formulated. There may be other ways but I know this method works. It is based on 10 years experience working with small and large organizations in sizes ranging from 200 to 200,000 people, both profit and not-for-profit.

The Leadership Conference Planning Process

LCPP might be called a fifth-generation planning process. The first generation is *the CEO's unwritten plan.* In effect, the CEO says, "I have a plan in my head, don't worry about it." The major problem with an unwritten plan is ambiguity in execution, and the resulting cost is wasted energy.

The second-generation process, *the plan written by the outside consultant,* appears to be a solution but is actually the worst possible choice. There's no management ownership or commitment to the plan and therefore no drive to implement or measure performance. An appropriate role for an outside consultant does exist, but that role is facilitating plan development as a skilled and objective outside agent.

The third-generation process is *the corporate planning department's plan.* It is a step in the right direction in that it is written, explicit, and sometimes has knowledgeable authors. I say sometimes because too often the planners are recently hired MBAs or people from outside the company who aren't knowledgeable about the industry or the firm. And even if the corporate planning department is knowledgeable and committed, danger exists in separating strategy development from implementation, which is always in the hands of the operator.

The fourth-generation planning process involved *delegation of the planning responsibility to key operating executives.* This was another step in the right direction, because strategy development and implementation were *both* placed in the hands of the operator. That results in a high level of ownership and commitment by each operator to his or her section of the plan. But this type of process assumes that the whole is equal to the *unlinked* sum of the parts. It leaves open the question of who is responsible for the corporate vision of the future and how commitment to that vision is forged. It also leaves open the question of how knowledgeable the operators are regarding each others' plans and how committed they are to addressing their interdependencies.

As a state-of-the-art process, LCPP draws on lessons learned from the flaws in prior generations of planning processes. LCPP is a carefully orchestrated series of conferences attended by the leaders of the corporation. The CEO does not merely approve the vision or just participate in its formation; he or she leads the process and manages the debate.

The process is *highly* participative. But as Max DePree, the former CEO of Herman Miller, says, "Participative management is not democratic. Having a say differs from having a vote."[1] Herman Miller's participative process does something right. It is the only company with sales of less than a billion dollars that has been twice named to *Fortune*'s 10 Most Admired Companies in the U.S.

In terms of management style, LCPP best fits the collegial (consensus, group-oriented) style of organization. It provides an excellent bridge for the personalistic (individual, self-oriented) organization that wishes to become more collegial, and for the formalistic (structured, hierarchal) organization interested in changing to a more open style.

Rx for Leaders No. 1   Don't let anybody else, outsiders or insiders, develop your vision or plan, no matter how proficient they may seem. They don't have the knowledge or the commitment.

Selection of the Core Group

"Unlike the vision of a founder-entrepreneur, visions in large complex organizations tend rarely to be one person's dream but rather the expressed commitment of a group."[2] I would expand on this statement: Vision is enhanced if it is the "expressed commitment of a group," regardless of the size of the organization.

The selection of participants in vision development is the first step in tailoring LCPP to a particular organization. The Conference Board (a nationwide association of businesses to improve the business system and to enhance the contribution of business to society) makes an explicit suggestion: "Faced with such uncertain times, today's chief executives believe that the way the corporation as a whole is most likely to survive and prosper is through the *ongoing involvement and support of all of the company's line operating executives* in formulating and implementing suitable business strategies."[3]

The Conference Board also offers some good general guidelines as to the number of participants needed in the LCPP process. Regardless of the size of the corporation or organization involved—General Motors,

---

[1]Max DePree, *Leadership Is an Art*, Doubleday, New York, 1989, pp. 22–23, with permission.

[2]Noel M. Tichy and Mary Anne Devanna, *The Transformational Leader*, John Wiley and Sons, New York, 1986, p. 128, with permission.

[3]The Conference Board, "Developing Strategic Leadership," Report No. 847, *The Conference Board*, January 4, 1989, p. 1, with permission.

the U.S. Army, or a small liberal arts college—three to five people set the goals and policies and determine future strategy. This certainly fits with my own business and consulting experience. The Conference Board goes on to emphasize that there are another five to ten executives in any organization who are so key to plan implementation that they must be included in the original formulation. If not, there will be a high risk of failure in implementation. Combining the two groups results in a group of eight to fifteen people. I call this small group the *core group* for vision formulation. The actual process of selecting the core group can give some insight on how the system works.

In October 1988 Bill Ruckelshaus, the former director of the Environmental Protection Agency became chairman and CEO of Browning-Ferris Industries (BFI), the $3 billion waste collection and disposal firm. As the new man on the executive team leading a very successful and high-growth organization, Ruckelshaus felt it was an ideal time to call everyone together and formalize a corporate vision to ensure continued profitable growth in the future.

The selection of BFI's president and chief operating officer, as well as the vice chairman, as members of the core planning group was quite simple. Ruckelshaus, together with these two, established corporate strategies and goals. Key implementors included other inside board members (the chief financial officer, the chief legal officer, and one of the regional vice presidents). The senior vice presidents of market development and disposal systems were also added, as was the corporate vice president for external affairs with responsibility for regulatory and environmental compliance. Finally, two additional regional vice presidents were added in keeping with Browning-Ferris's dedication to a decentralized operating style with heavy emphasis on regional autonomy. The core group totaled 11 members.

By way of comparison, consider Pratt & Lambert, Inc., a $250 million coatings and adhesives company. As the new CEO, Jerry Castiglia assumed the leadership role. Steve Stevens, chairman of the board and former CEO, sat in on all three conferences as an active participant.

Pratt & Lambert was organized around six operating divisions, each with its own president. The six presidents brought the number of participants to eight. Six corporate staff members also participated. Pratt & Lambert, like BFI, appointed a planning coordinator who handled all administrative matters for the core planning group throughout the session. The coordinator in each instance was a middle manager with high future potential who would likely benefit from the experience.

Both the BFI and Pratt & Lambert groups fell within the normal core group range of eight to fifteen members, although BFI is roughly ten times Pratt & Lambert's size. While a group of eight to fifteen is ideal, the process will work with as few as seven or eight members, and has worked with as many as fifty at The Continuum Corporation, a software firm based in Austin, Texas. At Phillips Petroleum, CEO Pete Silas decided that he wanted all his officers and senior managers to have a feeling of ownership of the resulting vision. His group totaled over 30.

Before the first meeting begins, the CEO must separate the participants into at least three teams. One team, called the *meld* team, is made up of the top three to five leaders of the corporation who generally set its direction, policies, and strategies. (In BFI's case, this included the CEO, the COO, and the Vice Chairman.)

The other members of the core group are split into two teams balanced as much as possible in terms of line-staff, headquarters-field, and so forth. If there are more than fifteen members of the core group, additional teams should be established to keep each team to fewer than six members for effective working purposes. The two teams are generally referred to as the *drafting* teams, since they will be responsible for preparing a first draft of each element of the corporate vision.

Rx for Leaders No. 2 Get all your senior executives involved in vision development, particularly your operating executives. Include not just the three to five who generally set policy, but the other five to ten who are key to its implementation.

LCPP Overview

The LCPP process is based on the philosophy that *planning must be done by the key leaders* of the organization, the same people who are responsible for implementation. Corollary elements of this philosophy are:

- Outsiders do not possess the knowledge or commitment.
- Outsiders cannot write plans for clients, but they can help clients write plans for themselves.
- Financial targets are important (they can be a driving force), but they are subordinate to the vision and values of the organization.

These guidelines are extremely important. The people within the organization who are responsible for plan implementation are also the people who must write it. The plan must be their own creation and one that they feel they own entirely. No staff group and no consulting group can do it for them.

An overview of the leadership conference planning process (LCPP) is shown in Fig. 5-3. As indicated by the time line at the bottom of the fig-

Leadership Conference Planning Process (LCPP) Flow Chart

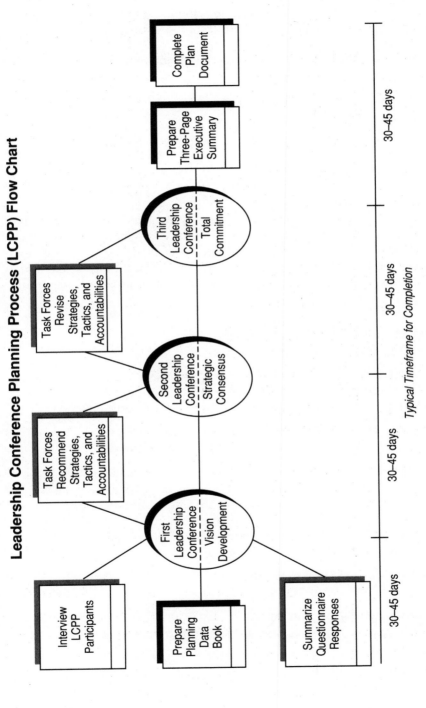

Interview LCPP Participants

Prepare Planning Data Book

Summarize Questionnaire Responses

First Leadership Conference
Vision Development

Task Forces Recommend Strategies, Tactics, and Accountabilities

Second Leadership Conference
Strategic Consensus

Task Forces Revise Strategies, Tactics, and Accountabilities

Third Leadership Conference
Total Commitment

Prepare Three-Page Executive Summary

Complete Plan Document

30–45 days   30–45 days   30–45 days   30–45 days

Typical Timeframe for Completion

Figure 5-3.

ure, 4 to 6 months is the typical timeframe for completion. This allows for a due period of deliberation before completion, and at the same time maintains proper momentum.

The process is based on three separate leadership conferences separated by approximately 30 to 45 days. Each conference also has its own specific purpose or theme:

Conference one	Vision development
Conference two	Strategic consensus
Conference three	Total commitment

Even before the first preparatory steps of the process are initiated, the CEO should hold a brief introductory meeting for all the core group members. This meeting will include an overview of the LCPP process and its underlying philosophy, as well as the reasons for defining or redefining the organization's corporate vision at this particular time in its history.

Guidelines for Developing the Corporate Vision

There are some general guidelines for developing the corporate vision and strategic plan that were laid down by George Steiner (one of the founding fathers of strategic planning and a professor at UCLA):[4]

- The chief executive must participate in, approve, and manage the enterprise on the basis of a network of aims [corporate vision].

This means that the CEO must do more than approve the plan. He or she must participate in and ultimately shape the key elements of the corporate vision; manage and guide the debate among the senior managers of the corporation; and, finally, be seen as managing the corporation based on the corporate vision—or the managers and people will recognize the whole process as a sham.

- Purpose, objectives, and goals should be written for the best calculated impact on decisions.

An unwritten vision and strategic plan is unacceptable. There is too much danger of ambiguity and inefficiency in the use of critical corpo-

[4]George A. Steiner, "Comprehensive Managerial Planning," Planning Executives Institute, 1971.

rate resources. Rather, it must have structure and be as graphic as possible to maximize understanding and commitment.

- Managers throughout the enterprise should participate in the establishment of objectives and goals for their own performance.

In a multibusiness organization, each business should have its own vision statement and supporting strategic plan.

- Aims should be realistic, reasonable, and challenging to the people in the enterprise.

At IBM, aims are designed to be "challenging but achievable." A vision, as a statement of strategic intent, should have an appeal beyond that of numbers and may even seem beyond our grasp at the present time, as long as the leader can demonstrate that the initial steps are achievable.

Remember that it is the leader who has the responsibility to develop a vision for the organization. It can be shared but not delegated. Participation by others is always desirable. Preparing the participants is our next task.

Rx for Leaders No. 3   Participate in and shape the key elements of your corporation's vision. Manage and guide the debate among your senior managers. Ultimately you must be architect and master

---

Rx for Leaders No. 4   Remember that participative does not mean democratic; having input doesn't mean having a vote.

6

Preparing the Core Group

The first step in the leadership conference planning process (LCPP) is a confidential questionnaire to be filled out by all members of the core group to assess their perception of the organization and its environment. The objective of the questionnaire and a subsequent interview is to initiate strategic thinking prior to the time the core group walks into the first meeting. Otherwise, the core group simply attends the first meeting in a reactive mode waiting for the CEO to take the lead. What you want is to put all attendees in a proactive mode, with each one having given considerable thought to the organization and its future, and having nurtured a desire to share in determining that future.

The Confidential Questionnaire

My suggested questionnaire (see Fig. 6-1) addresses the following critical areas:

- Significant accomplishments and shortfalls in the organization's past (Questions 1 and 2)
- Strengths and weaknesses of the organization at present (Questions 3 and 4)
- Opportunities and obstacles expected in the future (Questions 5 and 6)
- The most significant external factors (Question 7)
- The major markets served (Question 8)
- Achieving continuing vitality and growth (Question 9)
- The most critical tasks (Question 10)

1. What have been our major accomplishments over the past five years? What action can we take to leverage these accomplishments?

2. What have been our major shortfalls over the last five years? What action can we take to minimize the impact of these shortfalls?

3. What are our major strengths? How can we capitalize on these strengths strategically and operationally?

4. What are our major weaknesses? How can we correct them or minimize their impact?

5. What are the major external factors—*economic, political, regulatory, market, demographic, and competitive*—that will affect us over the next five to ten years? What actions can we take to effectively deal with them?

6. What are the major opportunities that lie before us in the next five to ten years? What can we do to capitalize on these opportunities?

7. What are the major threats or risks to our continued growth over the next five to ten years? What can we do to resolve them or contain their impact?

8. What are our major markets now served? Are there additional markets which should be served? If so, which markets and why?

9. What must we do to achieve continuing vitality and growth? Are new directions required? What are they? Why are they needed?

10. What are the three most important tasks which we face over the next 10 years? Why are they important?

Figure 6-1. Confidential pre-conference questionnaire.

The questions are about equally balanced between internal and external factors. However, this balance has not always been visible in the management of American business. As Peters and Waterman explained in their book *In Search of Excellence:*

> In marked contrast to the prevailing wisdom today, management theorists of the first sixty years of this century did not worry about the environment, competition, the marketplace, or anything else external to the organization. They had a "closed system" view of the world. That view, myopic as it now seems, centered on what ought to be done to optimize resource application by taking into account only what went on inside a company. It didn't really change much until almost 1960, when theorists began to acknowledge that internal organization dynamics were shaped by external events. Explicitly

taking account of the effects of external forces on the organization's internal workings, then, launched the "open system" era.[1]

The CEO forwards the questionnaire to each member of the core group. This gives the CEO a second opportunity, after the introductory meeting, to emphasize the particular rationale for initiating the LCPP at this time. As indicated in Fig. 6-2, a CEO's sample letter of transmittal, the completed questionnaires are summarized question by question. For each question, similar responses from members of the core group are brought together under a one-line "issue statement" to indicate the relative strength of the observation. Figure 6-3 shows a portion of a sample questionnaire summary. The percentage at the left indicates what portion of the core group addressed the one-line "issue statement." Back-up pages include the participants' exact comments as quotations without attribution. The back-up comments also include each respondent's proposed actions to build on positive factors and to minimize or correct negative factors. The summary of the questionnaires will become the initial discussion topic at the first leadership conference.

The summarization of the confidential questionnaires is a task requiring a high level of objectivity. It is the first of several tasks key to the success of the core group that will be performed by the plan facilitator. Other tasks include conducting the confidential interview of each member of the core group (which will be described next), and playing a key role in each of the three conferences and in the stewardship process that begins when the plan is completed.

Qualifications include extensive experience as a facilitator, the trust of the CEO and core group, and a background as a broad business generalist with a high level of objectivity. The task can be performed by an insider but is more easily handled by an outsider. For the CEO to do this is extremely difficult but not impossible. The plan coordinator, mentioned earlier, works with the facilitator to ensure that conference arrangements and administrative matters run smoothly. See Fig. 6-4 for a summary of responsibilities.

Rx for Leaders No. 1   Initiate strategic thinking before the core group walks into the first meeting. Get them in a proactive mode rather than a reactive mode simply waiting for you to take charge.

---

[1]Thomas J. Peters and Robert H. Waterman, Jr., *In Search of Excellence*, HarperCollins, New York, 1982, p. 91, with permission.

TO: Participants in the Leadership Conference Planning Process
FROM: Your CEO
SUBJECT: Corporate Vision Statement and Strategic Plan
Confidential Pre-Conference Questionnaire

You have been selected to participate in the development of a corporate vision statement and supporting strategic plan. The corporate vision will include our unique business mission, our distinctive values and beliefs, and our long-term business goals. Of equal importance is the development of closely linked strategies and tactics with a monitoring system for measuring our progress as well as a supporting financial plan.

The development of a corporate vision statement and strategic plan will serve several objectives. It will:

■ Provide an overall statement of business values, purpose, and strategic intent extending throughout the company.

■ Provide an interrelated network of values, mission, goals, strategies, tactics, and accountability statements that address every element of the business.

■ Provide a vehicle for improved communication of future direction to critical internal and external constituencies, including our board, managers, and employees, as well as our shareholders and the investment and financial community.

■ Provide a basis for improved allocation of business resources, both human and financial.

There is one other factor of note. We have enjoyed exceptional success as measured by high growth in revenues and earnings and consistently superior returns to our shareholders. But continued success cannot be automatically assumed or guaranteed. We must adapt to a changing business and regulatory environment. The key members of our management team need to participate in the establishment of long-range goals as well as short-term tactics. This is the best way to ensure commitment.

The work begins with the enclosed questionnaire. I would like your candid response to each question. Your responses should be from an

Figure 6-2. Questionnaire transmittal letter.

overall corporate or general management point of view. Take time to think about each question before you respond. Feel free to comment on any issue you feel is important at the end of the questionnaire. You are being asked to sign your questionnaire, so that we can monitor the returns. Names will not be used in verbal or written reports and individual responses will be confidential.

We would like to have your questionnaire returned as early as possible, but no later than [DATE]. Individual interviews will also be scheduled. A summary of our responses will be provided at the first conference which is scheduled for [DATE].

Sincerely,

Figure 6-2. (Continued)

The Confidential Interview

Some people are more comfortable with the written word and others are more comfortable with one-on-one conversations. That is why both channels of communication are provided prior to the first conference. The second step in preparing each member of the core group for the first conference is a confidential interview by the facilitator. The interview, approximately an hour in length, provides an opportunity to probe responses, clarify issues, and assess individual attitudes. As important as the information content in these interviews is the personal content, the opportunity to establish individual contact with each attendee prior to the first meeting.

Another function of the interview is to emphasize the role of the participants. It is extremely important that people do not wear their functional or operating hats at this meeting. All participants are there as extensions of the CEO with total purview of the organization. Since the responsibility or purview is total, attendees also are encouraged to address any aspect of the organization they wish, just as the CEO is challenged (and responsible) to address any part of the organization. This role is contrary to normal corporate manners, but it is essential to put aside parochial interests and limitations in view of the task at hand. Everyone must wear his or her corporate hat.

Q1   What have been our major accomplishments over the last five years? What action can we take to leverage these accomplishments?

        50% Maintained high quality or service image

        41% Maintained market share

        41% Effectively developed and introduced new products

        41% Improved sales or marketing efforts

        33% Enhanced awareness of need for cost reduction

        33% Improved or maintained profits and awareness of importance of profitability

        33% Established a strategic direction

Q2   What have been our major shortfalls over the last five years? What action can be taken to minimize the impact of these shortfalls?

        58% Inadequate new product introduction

        41% Inability to generate increased growth

        33% Absence of team concepts

        33% Complacency or deficient management style

        33% Inadequate cost reductions

        25% Inadequate technology

Figure 6-3. Questionnaire summary.

Rx for Leaders No. 2   Encourage the core group to address any aspect of the organization. This violates normal corporate manners, but it is essential to put aside parochial interests. Let the group know that everyone must wear his or her corporate hat.

The Planning Data Book

An important criterion for success by the core group in their visionary task is shared knowledge of the corporation and its business environ-

- Primary contact with facilitator.
- Arranges for distribution of Pre-Conference Questionnaire.
- Assists in arranging interview schedule.
- Arranges for meeting facilities, audio-visual aids, meals.
- Coordinates meeting agenda.
- Arranges for typing and distribution of worksheets generated during management conferences.
- Assembles common planning data book for Leadership Conference participants. A list of suggested tabs for the book is included below:
  - General
  - Market Studies/Competition
  - Current Budget and Planning Documents
  - Situational Analysis/Summary
  - Guidelines/Examples
  - First Meeting
  - Second Meeting
  - Third Meeting

These can be abbreviated or you may add or delete as appropriate.

Figure 6-4. Leadership conference planning process guidelines: the role of the planning coordinator.

ment that is as equitable and complete as possible. This is the purpose of the planning data book, which is compiled by the planning coordinator. (A 2- to 3-inch ring binder is usually sufficient to include all planning data materials.) It includes the summary of questionnaire responses, and provides a key source of input at the first meeting—an overall situational analysis ("where the corporation is today") based on the personal observations of the core group. But this summary is only qualitative in nature and a matter of internal management opinion. More is needed in preparation for the first meeting.

The planning data book also includes pertinent operating and performance reports, as well as financial statements and budgets. It contains any other critical information such as minutes of meetings, results of special studies or reports, and any external strategy audits or competitive analyses that are available. The CEO will usually make the final decision on what materials should be included in the planning data book. Some of the information may have been available only to the CEO and a few others prior to this time. Now all participants will share the same database. Information excepted includes items of extreme confidentiality, such as personnel records or acquisition or divestment matters pending at the time and whose disclosure would be inappropriate.

In addition to the normal operating, financial, and competitive data, the data book should include a gathering of relevant historical information and documents on the company's ethics, culture, policy, and practices. It should be prepared and distributed to the participants at least a week before the actual meeting to provide appropriate time for review and assimilation.

CEO Reservations

Generally, the CEO does not respond to the questionnaire personally. CEOs know their own feelings about the corporation. What they are interested in is the opinions and insights of the other members of the core group. The CEO's interview also is different from the others. It is more of a personal briefing by the facilitator, which ideally will help the CEO get the pulse of the group, know what to expect, and so on.

The CEO may have some reservations as the process begins, some of which will come out in the interview or during the conference itself. Some relate to the normal caution regarding a first experience, or perhaps unique characteristics of the business or institution, the adequacy of market analysis, or some other traditional aspect of planning.

However, the reservation that you might expect to be most dominant, at least from the CEO's perspective, has never been raised. It is an uncertainty related to a highly participative process: Does acting as a mere participant downplay the role of the CEO? Isn't the CEO supposed to lead, take the initiative, and lay out a vision for the others to approve? The meetings are structured in such a way that the participants always speak first and the CEO speaks last. While that always puts the CEO in the position of ultimate control, it is somewhat contrary to the perceived standard corporate practice. All of this is reviewed with the CEO ahead of time. Not once has there been a question, objection, or reservation raised.

In actual practice, CEOs seem to like participative input before they must take a position. It gives them the opportunity to hear two, three, or even more perspectives before a consensus begins to take shape. In some cases, group perspective is so much in agreement with the CEO's personal position that no overt decision is required. The veto is always there, but is seldom needed or used.

> **Rx for Leaders No. 3**   Provide the core group with all the pertinent background information and data available. Knowledge is power, and without equal knowledge the participants do not have equal power.

Group Reservations

Reservations on the part of the other members of the leadership group are varied: the "here we go again" feeling, the fear of being too open about or too critical of the boss, and concern about lack of adequate market analysis.

Few people in today's corporate world have not had a strategic planning experience. A great number are not enamored of that experience and are not anxious to go through it again. The questionnaire and the interview go a long way toward dispelling their reservations. It is clear from the questionnaire that participants' opinions are solicited and clear from the interview that the participants' role is much broader than any they have ever played before. In short, this process is different. There is usually considerable anticipation by the beginning of the first meeting. At the very worst, the attendees are open to persuasion that this process might lead to something.

Another leading reservation on the part of the core group is the fear of being too open about or too critical of the boss. At one opening conference, there was a discussion of several of the comments that were highlighted in the summary of the questionnaire responses. The discussion became quite critical regarding mixed signals coming from the CEO and the COO. Two participants got so concerned about what they had said, and how it was said, that they were quite worried about how it would be received. Everyone wondered what would happen when they showed up for work the following Monday.

Absolutely nothing happened. The company had just gone through a major merger, and the CEO had come from one side and the COO from the other. Their acceptance of the negative comments as being well meant created a new level of trust among the leadership group, whose members came from both sides of the merger. This is just one example of creating trust and displacing fear of candor. There have been many others.

Yet another possible reservation on the part of some participants is that the conference will lack technically professional market analysis.

The development of a corporate vision and supporting strategic plan will undoubtedly call for more information and special studies, but this should not delay the formulation of the vision or the strategic plan. Instead, such studies should be included as specific tactics and accountability statements in the strategic plan itself, with responsibility indicated for preparation and time for completion. Otherwise gathering market data could take an eternity, particularly in large corporations where the number of markets served is almost endless. In the final analysis, the core group will find their aspirations to be far more significant in constructing their vision and strategic plan than any market data.

The primary task of the core group is to produce a compelling corporate vision statement and supporting strategic plan. Market analysis is just one of the techniques available—and there are many others—that a group can use to develop their vision and plan. The questionnaire itself and the responses provided by the core group provide a very expert situational analysis that represents the best judgment of the group on both internal and external factors, and more importantly, what they feel needs to be done to address these factors. The accompanying planning data book may also include special market analyses from either internal or external sources. The core group can then draw from the questionnaire analysis or the planning data book as they see fit. In short, planning tools and techniques must not displace more fundamental planning tasks. Formulating the corporate vision and strategic plan is the leader's number 1 job, shared with the core group.

It is interesting to note that a rather abrupt turnaround has occurred regarding market analysis and strategic planning. Prior to 1960 there was practically no recognition of the external environment. Corporate plans had an internal focus. Today some companies have almost replaced strategic planning with extensive market analysis processes.

Rx for Leaders No. 4   Dissolve any fears or reservations among the core group participants. Humor helps. So does listening and being candid about difficult situations. It is up to you to take the lead in this area.

The Evolution of Strategic Plans

It is clear, in looking back, that the early strategic plans of the 1950s were financially driven. They were essentially 3-to 5-year extrapolations of the budgeting process from which they sprang. In the mid-1960s and early 1970s, strategic plans became market driven as management began to examine the external environment extensively. Strategic plans now taking shape are vision and commitment driven—more focused on aspirations and strategies and specific tactics to realize those aspirations. These plans will not displace the earlier financial and market driven plans but rather build upon them. "Clear vision results from a profound understanding of an organization and its environment. The executive needs a practical knowledge of the dynamics of industries, markets, and competition and must recognize the potential of the corporation to influence and exploit those dynamics."[2]

This chapter has addressed how an understanding of the organization and its environment is produced by the core group through confidential questionnaires and interviews combined with analyses of relevant markets and the external environment. Armed with this understanding, all should now be ready for the first leadership conference. The strategic thought process has been initiated through the questionnaire, specific questions explored and roles outlined in the interviews, and shared information provided by the planning data book.

[2]From *Creating Excellence* by Craig R. Hickman and Michael A. Silva. Copyright © 1984 by Craig R. Hickman and Michael A. Silva. Used by permission of New American Library, a division of Penguin Books USA Inc.

7

The First Leadership Conference

Vision Formation

Aristotle said "the soul...never thinks without a picture." This chapter is about developing that picture for the soul of a corporation. It will be an accurate reflection of the aspirations of the corporation, the values it wishes to live by, and the goals it is committed to achieve. First, let us discuss the structure of the development process, which is focused on the three leadership conferences.

Wherever possible, the conferences should be held off-site, outside the corporate headquarters. Since the conferences are intensive and reflective, a quiet, nonresort atmosphere is most desirable. Freedom from telephones during all sessions (including breaks, if possible) is mandatory. Meals should be taken together as a group.

One workable schedule and mode of organization for the conferences is as follows. The first and second conferences are scheduled (by the conference agenda) to last a day and a half. All participants are advised that discussion will not be limited and that the conference could last a full 2 days. The actual length will often depend on the CEO's style on discussion closure, whether he or she tends to let discussions run on or to cut them off early. The third conference is scheduled for a day, with the warning that a second half day could be required, although it seldom is. The group will generally go overtime if needed rather than extend the conference another half day.

The style of all the conferences is open, participative, and structured like a workshop. Visuals are simple overhead transparencies of the facilitator's coaching presentations on each element of the corporate vision, and the work teams respond with simple flipchart responses. The emphasis is on content, not form.

Make Vision Formation the Theme

The theme of the first LCPP conference is *vision formation*—the formation of the corporate vision itself plus the formation of a more effective working body for the leadership of the corporation. The task of the core group attending the conference is to produce a draft of a corporate vision statement and make assignments for the preparation of a supporting strategic plan.

The conference begins with an informal statement by the CEO on the present state of the corporation, as well as his or her thoughts or insights on the corporation's future direction (see the sample agenda of Fig. 7-1). It is important that the statement be directional in nature and not so well formed or explicit it they undercuts the purpose of the process. (The second and third conferences, which we discuss later, begin the same way, with the statement of the CEO or leader on where the corporation is at that time, and his or her general ideas on future direction.)

It is important to understand the mindset of each member of the core group as the conference begins. The questionnaire and the interview have been aimed at getting them thinking. They will all have their own agendas or at least a broad expectation of the results of the overall process. It is important for each member and the CEO to hear these agendas verbalized in response to the facilitator's questions: What do you hope this overall process will help the corporation achieve? What are you personally hoping to get out of it? This will put everybody's agenda on the table, and the reaffirmation of key expectations challenges the group to achieve those expectations. It also gets everybody immediately involved in the planning process.

Coordination of the first conference from this point forward is given to the facilitator. The opening comments are followed by a refamiliarization with the overall LCPP planning philosophy and process, and the conference's anticipated results. The tangible results include a corporate statement of vision and shared values and a supporting strategic and financial plan. The intangible results are equally important. They include a renewed sense of teamwork on the part of the leadership group; a unique

---

**First Leadership Conference Planning Session
Theme: Vision Development**

Friday, November 1, 199X

8:00	Opening Comments	CEO and Members
8:30	Vision and Values (Presentation)	Facilitator
9:15	Questionnaire Responses: Discussion	Facilitator
10:00	*Break*	
10:15	Questionnaire Responses (continued)	
11:15	Values and Beliefs (Workshop)	
12:00	*Lunch*	
1:00	Values and Beliefs (continued)	
1:45	Mission Statement (Workshop)	
3:45	Definition of Goals (Workshop)	
6:00	*Adjourn*	

Saturday, November 2, 199X

8:00	Strategy Development (Workshop)	
9:30	Tactics and Accountability (Workshop)	
11:30	Inter-meeting Assignments and Concluding Comments	CEO and Facilitator
12:00	*Adjourn*	

Figure 7-1. First leadership conference planning session agenda.

management development experience for everyone, including the CEO; and an effective process for corporate leadership and learning.

The second matter of business following the initial remarks from the CEO and the facilitator is a summary of the questionnaire responses by the facilitator. This will allow the respondents to look in the mirror and see themselves, or at least their composite view of themselves.

Generally no one escapes without taking a few lumps in the questionnaire analysis. It is very important in summarizing the questionnaires that the respondents' direct quotations be used. Direct quotes can sometimes be quite brutal but arguments can be avoided by keeping sources anonymous. The CEO is not excluded from criticism and often takes as many lumps as anyone else. On the other hand, no one is expected to defend him- or herself. The observations may be valid or invalid from a purely objective point of view, but they represent the candid opinion of somebody in the group.

The presentation of the questionnaire analysis is followed by another quick round-robin of each member of the core group to uncover any observations they would like to make about the observations and to ensure that they feel they are representative. It is then time to move on. Later, as the group begins to build the vision and supporting strategic plan, members will reevaluate the comments made in the questionnaire summary and decide what, if anything, should be done about them.

The objective of the discussion of the questionnaire summary is to secure the core group's agreement that this composite situational analysis is a valid representation of the group's assessment of its current strategic position. The summary then becomes a general depository of ideas that can be drawn upon as needed to construct the vision or subsequent portions of the strategic plan.

Rx for Leaders No. 1   Turn your key leaders into an effective working team by using a participative planning process. At the same time, build a process for corporate leadership and learning.

Define Your Shared Values

Speaking as current CEO of Herman Miller, Max DePree says, "Leaders need to be concerned with the institutional value system which, after all, leads to the principles and standards that guide the practices of the people in the institution."[1]

The most important part of the first leadership conference is a series of workshops on corporate vision and its key components: values, mission, and long-term goals. One key workshop is to discuss the concept of shared values. The facilitator can provide limited introductory comments, namely: Values are qualitative rather than quantitative; values are fundamental to the culture of the organization; and values are not created by the core group but identified in the way the organization sees and conducts itself, or aspires to conduct itself. Different kinds of subordinate goals or values based on the Pascale and Athos model and the Peters and Waterman models (see Chapter 2) can be enumerated. Several examples should be provided; the facilitator might well choose IBM, Ford, Phillips Petroleum, or BFI.

The drafting teams are then sent to individual breakout rooms with copies of the introductory materials just presented to them. They are

---

[1]Max DePree, *Leadership is an Art*, Doubleday, New York, 1989, pp. 11, 12, 24, with permission.

given an hour and a half for discussion, identification of key values, and the preparation of a one- or two-page flipchart presentation to the CEO's team and the other drafting team. The drafting teams have no designated leaders; the responsibility for the development task and the presentation is rotated. Unless there are more than five members on the team, each person will make at least one presentation, since there are five individual workshops. The only other instruction that the teams are given is that they must choose a team name, preferably a humorous one. Since the session is very intensive (and therefore quite exhausting), every effort is made to keep the mood as light as possible. Above all, team spirit is encouraged and usually very animated.

While the drafting teams are working through this first session, the CEO's team does not have a specific assignment, although it will have one in all the subsequent sessions. This hour and a half can be used for a more in-depth analysis of the questionnaire summary; a review of different analyses in the planning data book; a review of the steps in the process so that the team becomes more familiar with what will happen in this conference and the subsequent two conferences; a discussion, or question-and-answer period, between the facilitator and the team; or a more general discussion among the members of the CEO's team.

When the two drafting teams have completed their assignments, the teams gather for presentations. The spokesperson for each team is given 10 to 15 minutes for a presentation and questions from the CEO's team or the other drafting team. The team name is always utilized and loud applause for all presentations is mandatory.

It is not unusual if the culture of the organization is well established to have three or four of the same specific values identified by both groups, even if the wording is a little different. But this is not often the case if the corporation is divided into several business units. It is then up to the CEO's team to put the two drafts together with their own input and develop a blended set of shared values. For this reason the CEO's team is called the "meld" team. The two-part process of draft, then meld, continues through the establishment of long-term corporate goals, supporting strategies, and related tactics and accountability statements.

Throughout this whole process, except for the opening comments in the morning on the state of the business, the CEO is allowed to listen before speaking. This reverses the more generally accepted U.S. leadership process. The core group as a whole listens first to how they view themselves through the composite questionnaire analysis. The two drafting teams then put forward their own ideas on the fundamental values of the organization. It is only then that the CEO and the meld team go to work. While the CEO goes last, the final product must and will belong to the CEO.

Robert Greenleaf puts it quite succinctly in *Servant Leadership* when he emphasizes the importance of listening to the leader: "True listening builds strength in other people."[2] Leaders really appreciate the opportunity to listen before they speak. In many cases the speakers espouse the position the CEO has already taken, but the speaker or speakers have much greater ownership and commitment if they feel that it was their idea.

Rx for Leaders No. 2   Listen to your people throughout this whole process. Listening to them will make them stronger. It doesn't diminish your leadership: it strengthens it.

Draft Corporate Mission and Goals

The same drafting, presentation, and melding process is then repeated with regard to the corporate mission and long-term goals of the organization. Instructions are given on the fundamental elements of the extended mission statement (see Chap. 2): the core mission; the golden goose, and business segmentation; the external growth strategy; and the long-term financial goal. Once again, a number of real-world corporate mission statements are reviewed with the group as examples. The whole discussion should not last more than 10 or 15 minutes. It is intended to be a simple, nondirective set of instructions, including several examples, that leaves the drafting groups maximum flexibility. Not all the examples will adhere neatly to the instructions, which demonstrates that businesses are different, that there can be legitimate differences of opinion, and that each organization should select the elements most appropriate for them.

While the drafting teams are at work on the mission statement, the CEO and the meld team will work on merging the two sets of values with their own ideas. They note common themes or concepts in the two presentations and then seek out wording that has special appeal. Somebody from the group acts as scribe, though generally not the CEO. The proceeding is somewhat slow at first and then gains momentum. Two or three versions might be required before one is achieved that the group feels comfortable with. The CEO generally takes the role of final arbiter and manages the debate.

When the drafting teams have completed their deliberations on the corporate mission, the CEO can present to the drafting groups the meld

---

[2]Robert K. Greenleaf, *Servant Leadership,* Paulist Press, New Jersey, 1979, p. 17, with permission.

team's version of the values and beliefs. If the values of the organization are well established (and if the meld team has done its job), there is often visible agreement in the group during the CEO's presentation. In rare situations the assent can be so strong in the first presentation that no subsequent changes are needed.

However, this is not usually the case with the mission, goals, and strategic plan. These are debated, argued over, modified, edited, honed, and polished as the group moves from the very broad mission statement to detailed tactics and accountability statements. Throughout the whole process an attitude of openness and willingness to revise is critical.

All the flipchart presentation pages can be taped to the wall so everyone can see the gradual evolution of their work and gain a sense of group accomplishment. The drafting teams' original efforts are placed next to the final draft of the meld team. The CEO presents the final draft to the overall core group at each step and is careful to note the origin of phrases from either of the drafting teams (or give the reason for the meld team's addition.) A tremendous sense of ownership can be developed at this stage. Every member of the core group should be able to see one of their individual phrases or thoughts in the final product. Personal ownership of those few phrases is easily converted into ownership of the total product. This ownership is then readily transmitted into commitment to the vision and accountability, as we will see in later chapters.

The process is highly iterative in these first days. As the mission is developed, it may cause additional changes in the wording of the values. The development of long-term goals can in turn cause slight modification in the mission or values, and so on through strategies, tactics, and accountability statements. What the group is searching for is a vision that both challenges and provides a conceptual road map. "A vision is motivating for two reasons. First, it provides the challenge for which the organization and its members strive; it is the reach for excellence and the source of self-esteem for the members. The second purpose is to help provide a conceptual road map or a set of blueprints for what the organization will be in the future. Utilizing the metaphor of erecting a building: The vision starts with the architect's renderings—the idealized project that inspires people to move ahead—and then specifies the particulars that will be needed to get there."[3]

The morning of the second day can be devoted to learning the fundamentals of strategy and tactic development (a review of the material covered in Chapter 4). The workshop format is used: an explanation

[3]Noel M. Tichy and Mary Anne Devanna, *The Transformational Leader,* John Wiley and Sons, New York, 1986, p. 128, with permission.

with examples by the facilitator, an assignment to the teams, and presentations to the combined group.

At the end of the first conference, the group will have reached agreement on a draft statement of values, mission, and goals—the three basic elements of the corporate vision. More importantly, that agreement has been translated into ownership. This is not yet true of strategy, tactics, and accountability statements. The first conference only provides a starting point for the development of a supporting strategic plan, the vehicle needed to realize the vision.

Rx for Leaders No. 3   Create a corporate mission and supporting goals that fit you, your people, and your joint aspirations. Convert that authorship into ownership.

Assign Task Forces

Each of the organization's long-term goals, generally three to five in number, is assigned to a task force. The CEO assigns one member of the core team as leader. One other member of the core team is then assigned to each task force. The leader and the additional core group member become the nucleus of each task force. They, in turn, are asked to select two to four additional members from anywhere in the corporation. The new members are selected because of their particular knowledge or importance to the implementation of the strategies and tactics supporting the particular goal involved. It is also a very deliberate move to expand ownership and commitment to another 5 to 20 key people in the corporation who were not in the original core group. The end result is the establishment of three to five task forces with four to six members each. They will then develop the proposed strategies, tactics, and accountability statements between conference one and conference two. Responsibilities for the next conference are reviewed, and the first conference can be adjourned.

The conference generally ends on a definite high: The future has been probed, better communication between the participants has been achieved, the corporate vision has been defined, the future game plan is becoming clear, and the CEO's leadership has been confirmed.

All the flipcharts from the first leadership conference, both those of the drafting teams and those of the meld team, should be saved and copied by the planning coordinator and made available to the various task forces. This is usually done at a special kickoff meeting between the first and second conferences, where the CEO and the task force leaders explain to the new members of the task forces what went on in the first leadership conference. They review the process, distribute the draft copies of the values, mission, and goals from the first conference, and review the guidelines and examples of the strategies, tactics, and accountability statements that resulted from the first conference. Other sources of information for the task force groups include the situational analysis prepared from the questionnaires and all the data accumulated in the planning data book. The addition of task force members who were not part of the core group approximately doubles the number of people with a sense of ownership in at least one part of the plan.

At separate meetings, the task forces can generally agree on a set of three or four broad strategies to support their assigned goal. The task force leader may then appoint a member or two to develop tactics and accountability statements for each strategy, or this may be done by the task force as a whole. A second task force meeting, and a third if necessary, should be held to review the overall set of strategies, tactics, and accountabilities before recommendations are made to the core group at the second conference.

The meld team also generally meets between the first and second conferences. Some teams reconsider the draft of the organization's values, mission, and goals, or review preliminary drafts of strategies and tactics from the task forces. In other situations, the CEO or the meld team will meet with a number of different constituencies in an effort to develop further input or secure further ownership of the draft vision statement. This is particularly important for not-for profit institutions. For instance, in a college the president might wish to meet with a faculty group, a student group, an alumni group, the board of trustees or overseers, representatives of the administration, a group of significant contributors, and so forth. In many cases the core group will already include one or two members of these constituencies, but the CEO knows that broader input early in the process is highly desirable.

When describing any process, such as LCPP, it is important to keep in mind why we chose the process in the first place and what we hope to get out of it. The process should never be seen as sacred and is always subject to change. It is the purpose of the process that is stable. In each chapter describing the conferences, there is a discussion of some fundamental aspects of planning philosophy underlying the process. This chapter develops the notion that corporate planning is essentially a learning process whose fundamental purpose is corporate growth.

Rx for Leaders No. 4   Keep the purpose of all your planning efforts unchanging—corporate growth and survival. All processes, including LCPP, are subservient to that purpose and subject to change.

Plan and Learn

It is important to reflect upon the task that the core group is undertaking and, more specifically, the fundamental purposes of planning. A recent article in the *Harvard Business Review*, entitled "Planning as Learning," developed the theme that planning is learning by the senior managers of the corporation. Managers' ability to learn and to act on the information generated through the planning process will determine their survival:

> Some years ago, the planning group at Shell [Oil] surveyed 30 companies that had been in business for more than 75 years. What impressed us most was their ability to live in harmony with the business environment....
>
> Some companies obviously do learn and can adapt. In fact, our survey identified several that were still vigorous at 200, 300, and even 700 years of age. What made the difference? Why are some companies better able to adapt?...
>
> Outcomes like these don't happen automatically. On the contrary, they depend on the ability of a company's senior managers to absorb what is going on in the business environment and to act on that information with appropriate business moves.
>
> In other words, they depend on learning. Or, more precisely, on institutional learning, which is the process whereby management teams change their shared mental models of their company, their markets, and their competitors.
>
> For this reason, [Shell] thinks of planning as learning and of corporate planning as institutional learning.[4]

Rx for Leaders No. 5 Make your company a learning organization. While learning can never be institutionalized, sharing information with your key operating executives is one of the key benefits of the LCPP process.

Grow and Survive

In the final analysis, the purpose of planning comes down to one word: growth, with survival as the reward—particularly in publicly held companies. As stated in the opening sentence of Chap. 1, life is a process of competition and ultimately selection. The company targeted by the cor-

[4]Reprinted by permission of the *Harvard Business Review*. Excerpt from "Planning as Learning" by Arie P. De Geus (March-April 1988), p. 70. Copyright © 1988 by the President and Fellows of Harvard College; all rights reserved.

porate raider is often in the bottom half or the bottom quartile of its industry grouping. The industry front-runners in growth and profitability are seldom picked off. Their stock price is too high, and the raider will have difficulty achieving higher performance levels than have been already achieved.

Even divestiture is directed toward growth. Divestment of one of a family of businesses represents the survival of the fittest and the reallocation of resources to the survivors. General Electric routinely asks its business unit managers to identify the 10 to 20 percent of their assets with the lowest return, for either profit enhancement or divestment. In this sense, divestment represents the timely disposition of the dead or near-dead. If it is not done on a timely basis, an external predator may dispose of the whole corporation. At times, divestment may have to include otherwise good businesses that are not strategic to the future of the corporation.

The relative emphasis a leader places on growth or survival at any point in time can be a delicate call. There is a time for grand strategy, growth, acquisition, and heavy investment, and there is also a time for regrouping, bottom-line planning, and divestment or pruning of the corporate portfolio. A leader must decide when to change the course and speed of the organization from growth to survival and back again. But in the long term, growth can best ensure survival. In the very large corporation, and to a certain extent in the small or mid-size corporation, the leader must look at the corporation as an overall ecological system. "Our thinking about growth and decay is dominated by the image of a single life-span....Seedling, full flower, and death...But for an ever-renewing society, the appropriate image is a total garden....Some things are being born, other things are flourishing, still others are dying."[5]

Rx for Leaders No. 6   Grow if you want to survive. Your job as CEO is to continually plan for growth.

---

[5]John W. Gardner, *Self-Renewal: The Individual and the Innovative Society*, 2d ed., W. W. Norton, New York, 1981, p. 5.

8

The Second Leadership Conference

Strategic Consensus

The draft of the corporate vision was completed at the first conference, and the various task forces have by now completed an initial statement of strategies, tactics, and accountabilities for each goal. In the second conference, both will undergo a thorough and iterative review for direction, specificity, and harmony.

Establishing Consensus As the Theme

The theme of the second leadership conference is strategic *consensus*. All task force reports should be submitted to the planning coordinator and distributed to the core group participants approximately 1 week before the second conference. The reports should not be lengthy since the task groups have been instructed to devise no more than three or four strategies for each goal and three or four tactics for each strategy.

At this point the core group's appetite is generally larger than its capacity to digest. There is a tendency for the work to become broad and exhaustive rather than direct and focused. The number of tactics can quickly become overwhelming. A combination of five goals, five strategies, and five tactics for each strategy can result in 125 tactics, which can be uncontrollable in terms of implementation and accountability.

A slightly more modest four goals, four strategies for each goal, and four tactics for each strategy will result in a more manageable 64 tactics. A further slight reduction will make the plan even more focused on that which is most critical.

Once again, the conference begins with the CEO's state of the business presentation (see the sample agenda in Fig. 8-1). The message is informal but keys the group back in to the purpose of the conference. While the coordination of the first conference was largely in the hands of the facilitator, the coordination of this conference should be shared between the CEO and the facilitator. Only the CEO and the members of the core group can work out the consensus required in this conference. The facilitator will simply help with the structure of the conference, keep the meeting moving, and direct it toward a successful conclusion.

Second Leadership Conference Planning Session Conference Theme: Strategic Consensus

Wednesday, April 24, 199X

8:30	State of the Business	CEO
8:45	Meeting Purpose and Agenda	Facilitator
9:00	Values and Mission	CEO/Facilitator
9:45	*Break*	
10:00	Summary Remarks	Task Force Leaders
10:15	Goal I	Task Force Leader
12:15	*Lunch*	
1:15	Goal II	Task Force Leader
3:15	*Break*	
3:30	Goal III	Task Force Leader
5:00	*Adjourn*	

Thursday, April 25, 199X

8:30	Goal III (continued)	
9:00	Goal IV	Task Force Leader
10:00	*Break*	
10:15	Goal IV (continued)	
11:15	Conclusion and Wrap up	CEO/Facilitator
12:00	*Adjourn*	

Figure 8-1. Second leadership conference planning session agenda.

He or she may also assume the role of devil's advocate with regard to the clarity, brevity, and measurability of the emerging strategic plan.

The first order of business of the conference should be another review of the corporate vision. This might entail a brief half-hour discussion, or it could stretch to a lengthy and sometimes controversial deliberation in situations when there has been a recent merger or when a change in corporate direction is being considered. The mission, values, and goals are again carefully scrutinized. The core group, with the encouragement of the facilitator, may now begin to look at the vision from the perspective of the various constituencies of the organization.

The corporate vision will become a public document. It will be studied and reviewed by your customers, managers and employees, board of directors, shareholders (in the annual report), critical industry and financial analysts, various regulatory bodies, competitors and prospective competitors, and so forth. Significant care is appropriate.

Warren Bennis captures the role of the core group with regard to their task in vision development very well and concisely when he says that the successful CEO (as part of the leadership group):

- Develops a compelling vision of the firm's future.
- Translates the vision into a reality by concentrating on the keys to success.
- Remains deeply involved at the very heart of things, spurring the actions necessary to carry out the vision.
- Motivates employees to embrace the vision.
- Constantly articulates the vision so that it permeates all organizational levels and functions, taking the organization where it's never been before.[1]

Rx for Leaders No. 1   Keep your constituencies in mind at all times as you develop your vision. How will your customers interpret it and react to it? Your people? Your board?

Making the Vision a Reality

Developing a compelling vision was the primary task of the first conference. The primary task of the second conference is to reach agreement on how the organization will make the vision a reality. It is im-

---

[1]From *Creating Excellence* by Craig R. Hickman and Michael A. Silva. Copyright © 1984 by Craig R. Hickman and Michael A. Silva. Used by permission of New American Library, a division of Penguin Books USA Inc.

portant to consider the dynamics of what has happened between conference one and two. First, the original core group has been divided into three to five independent task forces, which have undertaken and completed their work independently of each other. Second, many task force members did not participate in the original core group conference. There will be a great opportunity for divergence of opinion and direction in this kind of situation, but there also will be an opportunity for significant new input and ideas.

At this point, the core group must examine the suitability of the task force recommendations and bring those recommendations back into close alignment with the vision statement. Some people have called this second conference the "milling around meeting," in that a number of disparate ideas will be advanced and considered, and some uncertainty will be apparent before specific direction is taken. Others have dubbed the second conference "the adult help meeting" in that the task forces are generally given more direction and help than they want. Both names are accurate, and both functions are necessary. The CEO and the core group as a whole will ultimately bring the independent efforts into a relatively balanced and synchronous whole, but before that can happen, an initial divergence in opinions is almost inevitable.

Each of the task force leaders will be asked to give a 5-minute summary of what happened in their individual task force meetings and what process they used in arriving at their conclusions. This will give the entire core group an overview of what transpired between conference one and two.

Next, the first task force will begin its report. Its members should first address the goal *itself*, given to them by the core group at the end of the first conference. They may recommend a slight or a significant change in the goal or its wording based on their work in developing supporting strategies and tactics. The core group, and finally the CEO, must take a position on the goal statement or defer making any decisions until after a complete review of the supporting strategies and tactics has taken place. The next step is for everyone to review the three to five supporting strategies, how and why they were selected, how they fit with each other, and how they represent a major and lasting effort.

It is the next step, forming the detailed tactics or action programs, that will move the organization from the present toward its aspirations for the future. Since each tactic can represent months or years of human effort, it deserves the careful attention it now receives. The assignment of responsibility for each tactic must also be done with care, since the person responsible (a member of the core group or one of the task forces where ownership is strongest) must be committed to the task, either at this time or certainly before the third conference. This means good communication, acceptance of responsibility, and agreement to a given start date and completion date, with interim review points or milestones if the task extends beyond several months.

Reviewing each goal will take about two hours. The time should be considered well spent when task accomplishment may be measured in months or years.

As in the first conference, there should be applause for each presentation. (It is amazing what a little applause does.) There should also be a deliberate search for consensus after each presentation, using these questions: Do the strategies and tactics represent the organization's primary agenda? Have we missed anything? Are there any conflicts?

Generally, not until the second or third team begins its presentations will the overlaps and gaps between the task forces become apparent. The additional participation gained as the task forces were formed will now be somewhat offset by individual differences in direction, style, and pace, but that price is well worth the value gained in creativity, ownership, and commitment.

Rx for Leaders No. 2   Anticipate divergence during the process. The process is structured to allow divergence as well as to gain strength from resolving it and refocusing the group.

Preparing for Commitment

Consensus is both the theme and the objective of this second conference, and it takes place quite naturally as the conference progresses. The task force leader presents, the other members of the core group comment, and the CEO moves the group to consensus. At the end of the conference the CEO and the facilitator provide guidelines to the task forces for the final conference.

The last part of the conference is dedicated to preparing for total commitment, the theme of the third conference. A final discussion centers on the following questions: Are we really doing the *right* things and not just trying to do wrong things right? Have we missed anything? Are there conflicts we need to resolve? How are we doing overall?

The task forces will meet again between the second and third conference to revise their strategies, tactics, and accountability statements in line with input from the CEO and the core group at the second conference. They will also identify the key or prime tactic under each strategy for inclusion in the plan schematic or summary that will be discussed later. This is the beginning of a focus process to determine the key short-term and long-term priorities that the CEO will place special emphasis on. The task forces will be asked to estimate additional revenues and costs implied by each tactic. These will later be incorporated into an overall financial summary of the strategic plan supporting the corporate vision. The task forces will also be asked to outline any other assumptions critical to the accomplishment of the tactics included in their goal statement. These will later be compiled into an overall set of plan assumptions.

Before the end of the second conference, the leader of the financial task force will discuss the parameters of the supporting financial plan and the need for any input from the various task forces. This is the first time that any sort of integrated discussions on financial topics, such as business volumes, the P&L statement, the balance sheet, and funds flow, have taken place. The development of financial planning schedules will be initiated between conference two and three and will be brought to conclusion after conference three.

Rx for Leaders No. 3   Define your tactics with utmost care. They are critical to commitment and move the organization from where it is today toward its aspirations for tomorrow. Each tactic represents months or years of effort and is deserving of careful attention.

Maintaining Momentum Between Conferences

Between conference two and three, the CEO and the meld group once again will consult with their key constituencies with regard to developments in conference two. The task forces will then reconvene to complete their work, and their leaders will ultimately submit the revised strategies and tactics to the plan coordinator at least a week before the third conference. The plan coordinator must assemble the entire vision statement and supporting strategic plan for circulation to the core group several days prior to the third conference. The coordinator also circulates a listing of all the tactics sorted by person responsible, and another listing sorted by scheduled completion date. (See the LCPP Tactic Control Report, Fig. 8-2). The purpose of these two listings is to eliminate unnecessary overload on any one person or any one period of time.

Rx for Leaders No. 4   Use the strategic plan to integrate the major activities of the organization; to prioritize them in terms of urgency; and to pace them to ensure progress without risk of burnout.

LCPP Tactic Control Report

ITEM	DATE DUE								RESPONSIBILITY
	3Q92	4Q92	1Q93	2Q93	3Q93	4Q93	...	4Q97	
1. PEOPLE GOAL 1.1 BENEFIT EVALUATION									
1.1.1 Insurance—Lower costs 15%, improve disability	8/31								Supervisor, employee benefits
1.1.2 Compensation—Non-exempt at 110% local average			2/15						Director human resources
1.1.3 Vacation policy—Competitive with firms of size within 50 miles						11/30			Operations manager
5. PROFITABILITY GOAL 5.1 WORKING CAPITAL									
5.1.1 Inventory turnover increase to 6				4/30					Materials manager
5.1.2 Receivables—reduce to 42 days sales								10/15	Credit manager

Figure 8-2.

Evaluating U.S. Business Leaders: Wimps or Heroes?

Because today's executives and managers are bombarded by the media with negative messages about the decline of the U.S. economy and the superiority of the Japanese managers, the second conference might conclude with a discussion of what U.S. business does well. The discussion can emphasize the role each business and each employee plays in national and international competition. It may build on Paul Kennedy's *The Rise and Fall of the Great Powers* and the importance of a nation's economic engine to its position in the world's economy. The discussion should also focus on the United States as the leader in real industrial output per capita, adjusted for purchasing power, as shown in Fig. 8-3. Two prevailing themes should be: (1) leadership relative to other competitors is one of the basic measures of any company or national economy, and (2) vision and strategic planning are two of the most fundamental aspects of leadership. The major points in the discussion should include the following:

- The U.S. economy not only continues to be the biggest but has even kept its lead in the 1980s.

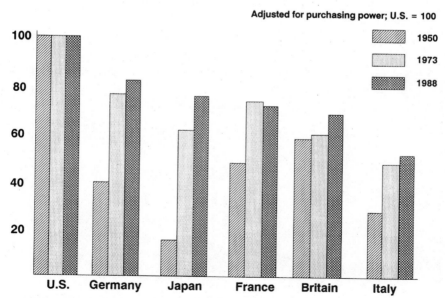

Figure 8-3. The leader in real output per capita.

- The real gauge of living standards is what a given amount of money in each country can purchase there.

- From 1980 to 1988 [the U.S. economy] has outpaced all other large industrial countries save Japan, which won by a whisker.[2]

[2]Rob Norton, "Still No. 1"—Economic Intelligence, *Fortune*, December 16, 1991, p. 24, with permission.

9

The Third Leadership Conference

Total Commitment

The first item on the agenda of the third leadership conference (see Fig. 9-1) is the corporate vision. This is the third conference at which it has been discussed, in addition to any discussions with various constituencies between the conferences. Closure and commitment at this stage are generally not difficult. By this time the group should tacitly understand that the corporate vision is particularly the responsibility of the CEO. The CEO has invited them to participate in its formulation but must ultimately take responsibility for its content.

Commitment As the Theme

The purpose of the third conference is achieving total commitment to the corporate vision and the strategic plan which will move them toward realization of that vision. This conference is generally a day or a day and a half in length, depending on the pace at which the CEO moves the agenda. At this stage, the CEO effectively becomes conference chairperson and the facilitator moves into the background. The tone is set by the CEO's state of the business comments at the beginning of the conference, which should express his or her expectations both for the day and the company's future.

	Third Leadership Conference Planning Process Theme: Total Commitment	
8:00	State of the Business	CEO
8:15	Meeting Purpose and Agenda	Facilitator
8:30	Vision Statement and Slogan	Joe Quigley
9:30	Goal I	Task Force Leader
10:00	*Break*	
10:15	Goal I (continued)	
11:15	Goal II	Task Force Leader
12:00	*Lunch*	
1:00	Goal II (continued)	
1:45	Goal III	Task Force Leader
3:15	*Break*	
3:30	Goal IV	Task Force Leader
5:00	Group Discussion	Facilitator
5:45	Concluding Remarks	CEO
6:00	*Adjourn*	

Figure 9-1. Third leadership conference planning session conference agenda.

It is then time for the task force leaders to present their supporting strategies, tactics, and accountabilities for each goal for final discussion and editing. Each of these discussions generally takes one to two hours. During this portion of the conference the CEO generally assumes a more directive role. Input has been sought, collaboration has been requested, but now some decisiveness and disposition are called for. Once again focus becomes paramount. Are all the tactics significant in terms of organizational health? Are they timely? This is the time to trim the fat, not add to it. Commitment is in the air. By this time, the leadership group is usually as anxious for closure as the CEO, since their ownership is real and their commitment has been sealed.

The group is now ready to move ahead to a discussion of the financial plan. While the financial plan is a vital third element (the first two being the vision statement and the strategic plan), the group is often less committed to it. They seem intuitively to understand that the financial plan is a desired result and not really the objective of the process. Their real commitment is to the vision itself and to the strategic plan designed to achieve it.

The conference concludes with a discussion of the outline of the ultimate plan document and the assignment of responsibilities. Generally, the ultimate plan document will have three parts: the corporate vision statement, the supporting strategic plan, and the resulting financial

---

Generalized Plan Outline

- VISION STATEMENT
  - Shared values
  - Mission
  - Goals

- STRATEGIC PLAN
  - Situational analysis (questionnaire summary, other analyses, etc.)
  - Strategies
  - Tactics and accountability statements

- FINANCIAL PLAN
  - Assumptions
  - Business volumes
  - P&L statement, balance sheet, funds flow, etc.

- SUPPORTING DATA AND APPENDICES

Figure 9-2.

plan (see the Generalized Plan Outline in Fig. 9-2). The vision statement will include values and beliefs, the extended mission statement, and long-term corporate goals. The supporting strategic plan will consist of the situational analysis (the original questionnaire summary and any other situational data from the planning data book considered important for inclusion) and the final strategies, tactics, and accountability statements generated by the core group. The financial plan consists of an overall statement of plan assumptions, a summary of expected business volumes, the related profit and loss (P&L) and balance sheet statements, and the highlights of the resultant fund flows. The appendix to the plan can contain any supporting data or information felt to be appropriate by the group.

The last item on the agenda in Fig. 9-1 is a group discussion, which can be kicked off by selected quotations from a recent special report by *Fortune* magazine: "What I Want U.S. Business to Do."[1] The quotations are highly supportive of the vision and strategic plan the group has just completed, and the journey they are about to undertake to realize their vision:

---

[1]"What I Want U.S. Business To Do In '92," *Fortune,* December 30, 1991, pp. 24–26, with permission.

> I would like to see you do what you do best. You can build on your
> enormous successes.   GEORGE BUSH

Your best chance for business success is to build on your core competence or golden goose. Stay focused. Don't dissipate your efforts. Abide
by the mission you have just completed.

> I would love nothing better than if President Bush stood up and said,
> "We are going to have a forum in this country for the next year, and
> we are going to decide what our basic values are and what our goals
> are for ten to 20 years out."   STEVE JOBS

You have done for your corporation what Steve Jobs wanted President
Bush to do for the country. Now is the time to communicate your values
to your people, your customers, and your vendors.

> But in times of crisis, change, and recovery, I've seen a number of or-
> ganizations go for a person with terrific ambition and terrific com-
> petence absent integrity. I call those destructive achievers. I think
> that's what we have to work on.   WARREN BENNIS

Walk your talk. Keep integrity ahead of ambition, even competence.

The purpose of the discussion is to celebrate the significance of the vision and plan formation task the group has just completed, as well as to
look ahead to the magnitude of the task now before them—successful
implementation. The fact that it may be 2 to 3 years before the plan and
planning process are "wired in" is temporarily set aside, along with the
fact that the process of achievement of their vision will probably continue for years.

> **Rx for Leaders No. 1**   Don't rest now. Communicating your new
> vision must begin quickly. Remember that it takes time and effort to
> get a vision and supporting strategic plan wired into the manage-
> ment team and the organization.

The LCPP: Distinctive
Features

Before moving on, it is important to look back and summarize the distinctive features of the LCPP, to recognize the LCPP's dependence as a
process on a more fundamental measure of strategic health, and to emphasize the support that the LCPP offers to the total quality manage-

ment (TQM) effort in any corporation. The LCPP process for building a corporate vision and a supporting strategic plan is really quite simple and does not depend on any special inspiration or on the charisma or writing abilities of a CEO. Rather, it depends on the shared talents of the leaders of the corporation to summarize concisely and in a compelling way what they aspire to be as a corporation, what they are committed to achieve, and the values they intend to live by. They must then share their vision with others, both inside and outside the corporation, and sustain that vision over a long period of time despite many challenges and obstacles. Sharing and sustaining the vision are the subjects of Part III of this book.

The LCPP has a number of distinctive features as a planning process:

- A clear, concise, and written corporate vision as the end product.
- A value-based foundation.
- A heavy market, customer, and competitive orientation.
- A high level of management consensus and commitment. This can only come from people working together on a conference basis, as opposed to working alone in individual offices.
- Tactics and accountabilities directly linked to the corporate vision and strategic plan. The tactics must lay out the path of implementation and provide a structure for accountability.
- A succinct and graphic plan summary. No matter how lengthy the plan may be, it must be possible to summarize it in not more than three pages, front and back. Furthermore, the plan summary must include graphics so those outside the core group can understand the overall plan quickly and clearly and commit its essence to memory—which is where you really want it in the first place. (See Figs. 10-1 to 10-5 in Chap. 10 for an example of a plan summary.)
- Adoption of the corporate vision and strategic plan as key elements of the overall management process, clearly recognized as such by lower levels of management. People must perceive the vision and plan as guiding and controlling management's actions.
- A planned and coordinated communication process or roll-out for the vision and strategic plan led by the CEO. We will discuss the roll-out process in Chapters 10 and 11.
- A well-defined stewardship and renewal process. A series of quarterly plan reviews and annual renewals, with clear emphasis on stewardship, keeps the vision alive and vital. We will discuss this in Chaps. 12 and 13.

> **Rx for Leaders No. 2**   Maintain a clear and concise corporate vision statement with a strong value and culture orientation. Then communicate it to your people and keep it vital.

The Fundamental Determinant of Strategic Health

While LCPP is a tested fifth-generation planning process and has many distinctive features, it will not work if the corporation loses sight of the fundamental determinant of the strategic health of the business. The determinant is not the profit and loss statement, or the balance sheet, or cash flow statement, or any so-called bottom line. These are all very valid indicators of the financial health of the business, but not necessarily of its strategic health. Rather, it is the customers' perception of your product or service relative to that of your competitors. Your profitability, balance sheet, and cash flow are determined by your customers' perception of your product or service relative to that of your competitors. In fact, certain criteria that help ensure strategic health might be called "The Four Cs of Corporate Strategic Health":

- *Customer Satisfaction.*   Everything starts and ends with the customer and is directed toward ensuring that he or she perceives your product or services to be superior.

- *Competitive Awareness.*   Thorough knowledge of competitors who have exactly the same objective that you do is essential. In fact, your desire for knowledge of your competitors should stop just short of paranoia.

- *Cost Effectiveness* in serving the customer. This doesn't mean being more cost effective as the product leaves the plant. It refers to cost at the point of use, whether of a product or a service. Cost accounting reports as we know them today are important but simply do not get the job done in terms of examining costs through point of use.

- *A Winning Culture.*   People must feel they are winners, deserve to be winners, and will settle for nothing less than being winners.

Directly linked to this winning culture is the corporate golden goose (discussed in Chap. 3) and the commitment to support it. This is the business that is most dominant and most profitable, as well as the area most likely to develop a winning culture.

Rx for Leaders No. 3   Recognize that LCPP (or any other process) won't work without a clear focus on the strategic health of your business—your customers' perception of your product or service relative to that of your competitors.

Rx for Leaders No. 4   Improve and maintain the strategic health of your business through the four Cs of business success: customer satisfaction, competitive awareness, cost effectiveness, and a winning culture.

The LCPP and Total Quality Management (TQM)

There are seven examination categories for the Malcolm Baldrige Award, which is given annually on a highly competitive basis to national leaders in "total quality." The first category examines the role of leadership in the search for continuous improvement. Subcategories of leadership include "senior executive leadership," "quality values," "management for quality," and "public responsibility." I can think of no better way of demonstrating executive leadership in the search for quality than the leadership conference planning process. It clearly positions the top leaders as providing the impetus for quality. Specific strategies supporting that goal can address the other key Baldrige examination categories: "information and analysis," "strategic quality planning," "human resource utilization," "quality assurance of products and services," "quality results," and most important of all, "customer satisfaction." The linkage between quality and customer satisfaction is clearly demonstrated.

The consensus goals of the 1990s (as explained in Chap. 1) are twofold: achieving total quality and empowering people. Total quality is seen as absolutely necessary to achieving high levels of customer satisfaction and lasting competitive advantage. The World Management Congress mentioned in Chap. 1 combined the two: *total quality through empowered people*—indeed, in the final analysis quality improvement can only be achieved through empowered people.

A recent IBM stockholder's report speaks both of quality and the people who create it:

> Quality topped the agenda at a meeting this January of IBM's senior executives from around the world. During the course of the meeting,

company management launched a comprehensive program designed to virtually eliminate defects from every IBM solution and business process...."Market-driven quality means understanding quality as our customers see it," said IBM Chairman John F. Akers....To this end, the company is establishing measurements that reflect the views of the marketplace on IBM's offerings and services. These measurements will allow the company to better direct the efforts of its employees, vendors and Business Partners to deliver world-class solutions.[2]

Later that year, IBM was one of four companies in the nation that received the Malcolm Baldrige Award for outstanding quality in another example of achievement following clear goal setting and commitment. It doesn't just happen effortlessly.

The Browning Ferris Industries (BFI) mission statement (examined in Chap. 3) placed a special emphasis on quality, which was to become the first among equals of the five BFI long-term goals. Bill Ruckelshaus, the CEO, took four of his top executives to a Conference Board seminar in New York City on total quality management while the BFI strategic plan was still under development. It was a dramatic way to emphasize the importance of their quality goal. Before BFI's strategic plan was a year old, Ruckelshaus also took the fourteen top BFI officers to Washington, D.C., for the annual awarding of the Malcolm Baldrige Award to the outstanding quality leaders in the nation. Quality is no longer a way of life at BFI; it is *the* way of life.

Rx for Leaders No. 5   Make total quality and empowering people your goals. In the final analysis, quality improvement can only be achieved through empowered people.

---

[2]IBM Stockholder's Report, first quarter 1990, p. 5, with permission.

PART 3

Vision, Communication, Stewardship, and Renewal

- Discusses how to communicate the vision through an effective "roll-out" process.
- Tells how to make the vision a reality through periodic review and renewal.
- Emphasizes the importance of sustaining the vision and values over time and through crises.

10

Communicating the Global Vision

The Short-Term Roll-Out

Even a compelling and global vision requires effective communication to generate consensus and commitment beyond the small core group of authors:

> Only through good communication can we convey and preserve a common corporate vision. Communication can sharpen, embody, and help enact that vision....An increasingly large part that communication plays in expanding cultures is to pass along values to new members and reaffirm those values to old hands. A corporation's values are its life's blood. Without effective communication, actively practiced, without the art of the scrutiny, those values will disappear....[1]

Rx for Leaders No. 1 Communicate the vision personally to your people. Get your PR people involved to gain their expertise. But don't delegate the task. Even a compelling global vision requires effective communication to generate consensus and commitment.

---

[1] Max DePree, *Leadership Is an Art*, Doubleday, New York, 1989, pp. 94–95, with permission.

Performance Report on
Strategy Communication

According to a corporate strategy study done by The Forum Corporation in 1989, "There are differences between CEOs and their direct reports on...the degree to which their corporate strategies are effectively communicated.

- Whereas 96% were confident in their strategic direction, only 74% of the respondents believed that their strategy was `understood by everyone who needs to know.'

- While 82% of CEOs believed their strategy was understood by others, this view was held by only 68% of the Chief Operating Officers, 62% of Chief Financial Officers, and 74% of Executive Vice Presidents.

- Among CEOs, 80% believed their strategy was `influential in their company's day-to-day operations.' Only 71% of COOs and 68% of CFOs agreed. (Although this study did not measure middle-management views, in The Forum Corporation's consulting experience, we routinely encounter significant doubt and confusion at this level of the organization regarding strategic direction.)"[2]

The letter to the editor of *The Wall Street Journal* on the boss's grand plan as summarized in Chap. 4 gives evidence of the doubt and confusion often encountered at the middle management level. In a separate study that explored the organization at a deeper level, Professor Robert E. Kelley of Carnegie Mellon University found that "The trust and loyalty of *gold-collar* workers have been eroded by poor management, few rewards and employers' failures to clearly communicate goals."[3] Kelley uses the term gold-collar workers to describe a new breed of employees and managers valued for their brain power. "It's clear that gold-collar workers aren't buying the management package—the goals, approach or management style—being offered to them....Nearly 66% of the respondents said their company's leadership failed to ensure a clear understanding of a corporate `vision, mission and goals' in its workforce."[4]

Rx for Leaders No. 2   Provide your people with the opportunity to see, hear, question, and discuss your vision for the future. Consensus and commitment generally fall off the deeper you go into the organization. Make certain you communicate your vision to everyone in the company.

---

[2]*The Forum Corporation Corporate Strategy Study* (The Forum Corporation of North America, 1989), pp. 2–3, with permission.

[3]*Survey of "Gold-Collar" Workers Shows Erosion of Trust, Loyalty*, Carnegie Mellon Department of Public Relations, Press Release, January 31, 1990, p. 1.

[4]Ibid.

Communication Is the Key to Commitment

The core group's planning and learning experience must be communicated until it creates meaning at all levels of the enterprise and in every geographic area of operations. Communication is one of the basic purposes of planning, and it facilitates another key purpose of planning—the creation of a clear strategic focus and a shared management vision that results in commitment and the will to act. It is communication that creates this shared vision and the will to act.

Planning has been characterized earlier as learning by the senior management of the organization. Leadership transmits learning to fix and secure the company's tradition.

> **Rx for Leaders No. 3**   Pass on your vision effectively to your people, or the work of the leadership group will be meaningless.

The Beginning of the Roll-Out

Roll-out in this context refers to the leader's responsibility to communicate the corporate vision and values throughout the organization. To quote Warren Bennis and Burt Nanus, "Communication creates meaning for people. Or should. It's the only way any group, small or large, can become aligned behind the overarching goals of an organization. Getting the message across unequivocally at every level is an absolute key."[5]

The wise leader will begin the plan roll-out after the first LCPP conference by informally reviewing the draft mission, values, and goals with all important constituencies with a request for formal or informal comments, and do the same after the second meeting with regard to strategies and critical tactics. The direction and thrust of the leader's vision should surprise no one by a dramatic unveiling at the end of the process. In for-profit organizations constituents are the board of directors, customers, suppliers, regulatory agencies, and so forth. In not-for-profit organizations such as colleges or universities, constituents are the faculty, administration, the board of trustees or overseers, students, alumni, benefactors, and friends.

[5]Warren Bennis and Burt Nanus, *Leaders: The Strategies for Taking Charge*, HarperCollins Publishers Inc. New York, 1985, p. 43. Copyright © 1985 by Warren Bennis and Burt Nanus.

Roll-Out Planning

Formal roll-out planning for the finalized vision statement and strategic plan begins during the third LCPP conference. Roll-out planning includes all aspects of the leader's responsibility to communicate the vision and strategic plan to everyone in the organization. Near-term aspects, such as vision presentation and documentation, are covered in this chapter, and longer-term aspects in the following chapter. Each element of the final plan is assigned to one person for continuing responsibility.

- The CEO has responsibility for the vision portion: the mission, values, and goals.
- Each goal remains the responsibility of the original task force leader (sometimes called "goal manager" or "executive") for completion, presentation, progress reporting, review, and subsequent revision.

There should be an open discussion of appropriate plan presentations, style, and responsibility at the third LCPP. In determining the number of plan presentations, remember that people cannot commit and contribute unless they have been informed. I would suggest overdoing the number of presentations rather than having too few. The core group has spent 4 to 6 months putting the overall vision and strategic plan together, and hearing the presentation twice is not going to hurt anyone. In fact, as the number of presentations increases, the audiences will probably be smaller and participation will be more likely.

A word of *caution:* Don't expect the audience to see the same magic in the words that you and the leadership group have found. The audience didn't participate. Furthermore, people may wait to see whether the plan changes the way things are done in the organization before they begin to give it their full commitment and support, so have patience. Hesitation should not be viewed with alarm, and the only remedy to the delay it causes is to make a visible change in the leadership group's actions. The bigger the cultural change called for in the vision, the longer the delay factor might be.

The responsibility for a plan presentation should always be shared.

- The leader should present the vision statement along with some of the rationale and discussion that took place in shaping it.
- Each of the task force leaders or goal managers should present the strategies, tactics, and accountability statements supporting their assigned goal.

"Visible announcements of opinion or intention greatly increase commitment to the chosen action."[6] My personal experience is that the core group itself becomes more committed to the vision and plan each time they present it. Speaking before your peers and subordinates does wonders in firming your resolve. With regard to presentation medium, I've seen very effective presentations made with an overhead projector or professional 35mm slides. It is important that the presentation fit the style of the organization.

Rx for Leaders No. 4   Don't expect your people to see the magic in the words that you and the core group have found. It's not their invention. Walk your talk and have patience.

Near-Term Tasks

There are several near-term roll-out tasks that must be performed shortly after the third meeting:

- Select a *key tactic* for each strategy.
- Determine the *executive short list*.
- Develop the *financial summary*.
- Complete the *three-page executive summary*.

Each of these tasks will be discussed in detail. The executive summary will be discussed last, since the other items are all elements of it.

Earlier, in discussing business segmentation, I commented that all businesses are not born equal. There is generally one business in a given corporation that best reflects the corporation's distinctive competence and contributes most to the bottom line. This is also true of one of the three to five tactics that support each strategy—one tactic is generally considered to contribute most to the achievement of the overall strategy. Each task force should be asked to indicate the key tactic for each strategy supporting the goal they are responsible for. This is generally represented in the complete document by an asterisk or some other indication.

---

[6]From *The Renewal Factor* by Robert H. Waterman, Jr. p. 304. Copyright © 1987 by Robert H. Waterman, Jr. Used by permission of Bantam Books, a division of Bantam Doubleday Dell Publishing Group, Inc.

An executive short list (Fig. 10-4) contains three to five short-term priorities and three to five long-term priorities that the CEO will place special emphasis on. The priorities should not be new. They represent a further distillation of the values, goals, strategies, and key tactics of the plan itself that will receive special emphasis over the coming year or so. The concept behind the short list began with John Nevin, the head of U.S. pharmaceuticals for SmithKline Beecham several years ago. Nevin wrote both his short-term and long-term priorities on the back of a card and carried it with him wherever he went. Each time he reached a goal, he crossed it off the list and refocused his energies on the remaining priorities. When he shared the list with his people, which he always did, it showed them what he perceived as critical. The short list helped Nevin and his managers, and it can help you too. Figure 10-4 contains a sample of an executive short list.

The financial summary (Fig. 10-5) deserves some explanation. Few chief financial officers—and even fewer of the people in the finance department—would accept a one-page summary as adequately addressing the corporation's finances. But for most CEOs and operating people, it is extremely useful, since it incorporates on one page the things that they have told us are most critical when looking strategically at the future.

The financial summary begins by examining unit sales, rather than net sales. This allows executives to examine the trends in key operating volumes without being confused by pricing and inflationary factors. Net sales, gross operating profit, and net profit compress the P&L to its essentials, while return on sales links the two key numbers. Average equity and return on equity relate the P&L to the balance sheet. And the final three items provide a look at the capital spending budget and what is happening from a cash flow point of view.

Horizontally, the financial summary provides 2 years of actual history with a current-year estimate and a 5-year historical compound growth rate. The forward years are projected individually together with a 5-year compound growth rate that can be compared to historical growth. This one-page summary could be backed up, and generally is, by thousands of detailed pages from the finance department.

Rx for Leaders No. 5 Make certain your vision and strategic plan dominate the financials. Don't let financials upstage your vision. Remember that the financials are just the projected results of vision achievement, not the vision itself. Numbers don't move many people.

The Three-Page Executive Summary

Figures 10-1 through 10-5 are examples of the three-page executive summary for the mythical ABC Corporation. Each of the elements has been discussed previously.

The format of the three-page executive summary can be summarized as follows:

- Page 1: Front—*Shared Values* (10-1)
  Back—*Mission* (10-2)

- Page 2: Front—*Plan schematic* (10-3)
  Back—*Plan schematic* continued if needed. (Each side can accommodate up to four goals, which should accommodate almost any strategic plan).

- Page 3: Front—*Executive Short List* (10-4)
  Back—*Financial Plan Summary* (10-5)

The importance of the three-page executive summary should not be overlooked. It is a key to plan clarity and execution for the core group and those working closely with them. The summary can also be critical to driving the completed plan down into all levels of the organization, and outward to appropriate constituencies.

The Need for Focus

The concept behind the three-page executive summary came from Charlie Strang, the retired CEO and chairperson of Outboard Marine Corporation (OMC). Strang and the OMC core group were sitting in the board room in 1981 as he described the coming invasion of the Japanese outboard engines from Yamaha, Suzuki, Honda, and Nissan. Defending OMC's 45 to 50 percent market share in the United States and 35 percent share globally would require focus and dedicated effort by everyone. Yet more than half the group felt that a merger with another company or diversification were their only viable alternatives.

Strang contended that the correct course was the exact opposite. It would call for a massive redesign of their complete product line, some method of reducing their labor costs by perhaps 50 percent, and keeping everybody's eye focused clearly on the ball. To Strang, diversification or a merger would result in just the kind of confusion and diffusion of energy that would give the Japanese manufacturers their chance to pounce on OMCs existing market share.

ABC CORPORATION
SHARED VALUES

We are dedicated to our:

CUSTOMER SERVICE:	Identify and service customer needs in a manner that will establish trust and loyalty.
EXCELLENCE:	Instill a sense of pride in excellence throughout the organization.
INNOVATION:	Maintain and enhance our tradition of innovation.
INTEGRITY:	Respect all individuals that the company touches.

Figure 10-1.

Strang felt that this focus needed to be represented in the document itself. He had in front of him a stack of three-ring binders that represented the plans of the various divisions. He was willing to devote a year of his time to developing a new global vision and strategic plan for OMC, but he felt the document should reflect the focus that he wanted. He didn't care how much backup material there was in terms of tactical detail or financial support, but he wanted the ultimate document to be no more than three pages.

Because he was an engineer, he believed the vision and plan should be graphic so that people could understand the relationship between the parts. He wanted to make sure that responsibilities were clearly defined and priorities were summarized and highlighted. He also wanted a financial summary, but one of no more than one page. That was a tall order for three pages, even when utilizing both sides.

As Strang described it, the three-page executive summary was intended to be short, simple, and graphic, and to assign responsibilities clearly. Looking at it another way, the summary was so compact that it could be folded up and put in your coat pocket or purse. Once the vision and plan were distilled to that extent, there was a good chance that the essentials could be remembered. And if the essentials are remembered, there is a whole lot better chance of implementation.

Ten years later, the results of Strang's insistence on focus in both documentation and implementation have been quite remarkable. OMC still has a 45 to 50 percent market share in the United States through its Johnson and Evinrude outboard engines. It also still holds a 35 percent

ABC CORPORATION
MISSION

We provide superior-quality industrial and commercial bearings and related support services to our customers. We aspire to be the performance leader in our industry and provide a superior return to our shareholders with particular emphasis on a team effort among our people.

The mission for each of the existing businesses is summarized below based upon anticipated potential to contribute to the above corporation's long-term goal.

- GENERAL AVIATION MARKET: Expand its present base to include commercial and military aircraft through the development and enhancement of metal and successor bearings. Enlarge this thrust to include the industrial and commercial transportation market. Develop the business on a national precision marketing basis.
- SELECTED MARKET SEGMENTS OF STRENGTH: Maintain or increase bearing market share. Develop as a national business. Market through the Bearings Division sales organization as well as the Southern Bearing sales organization.
- GENERAL INDUSTRIAL BEARINGS MARKET: Define and target selected segments on a regional, geographic territory basis.
- GSA—MILITARY SPECIFICATIONS BUSINESS: Develop on a national account marketing basis.

Pursue external growth opportunities aggressively:

- In the aviation/transportation and targeted high growth bearing market segments, pursue technology or proprietary position.
- In the general industrial bearing business areas, acquire and consolidate as appropriate for economy of scale in manufacturing and/or marketing.
- In the international market, seek additional licensing (buy/sell) agreements.

Our long-term financial goal is to achieve a total return to shareholders that establishes ABC in the upper quartile of our industry and U.S. industry as a whole.

Figure 10-2.

ABC CORPORATION
SHARED VALUES

CUSTOMER SERVICE   EXCELLENCE   INNOVATION   INTEGRITY

MISSION

We provide superior quality industrial and commercial bearings and related support services to our customers. We aspire to be the performance leader in our industry and provide a superior return to our shareholders with particular emphasis on a team effort among our people.

GOAL I

GROWTH
Ensure long-term growth and increase market share.

GOAL II

QUALITY
Guarantee customer satisfaction through continuous quality improvement.

GOAL III

PEOPLE
Increase productivity and opportunity through improved training and communication.

GOAL IV

SHAREHOLDERS
Achieve a total return in top quartile of our industry.

STRATEGIES

1.1 Structure sales and marketing organization to better address customer needs.
1.2 Increase sales of products in existing markets.
1.3 Pursue sales of products to new markets.

TACTICS & ACCOUNTABILITY

1.1.1 Install sales/marketing structure which aligns with product lines yet maintains current 10% of G&A expenses: Gen. Mgr. Mktg; B:10/93, S:4/94, C:12/94.
1.2.1 Achieve 90% or more of field sales force reaching 100% of sales targets: Sales Mgr.; B:6/93, S:9/93, C:12/93.
1.3.1 Identify opportunities in aircraft and/or transportation market which are likely to return above our average 3.6% ROS and which represent at least $10 million in new revenues: Mgr. Mkt. Research; B:12/93, S:3/94, C:9/94.

STRATEGIES

2.1 Implement feedback systems to ensure a high level of customer service.
2.2 Realign resources to effectively meet customer needs.
2.3 Provide an effective quality assurance program.

TACTICS & ACCOUNTABILITY

2.1.3 Administrate an effective, annual customer opinion survey, highlighting product improvements to achieve 15–20% response rate: Mgr. Mkt. Research; B:12/93, S:6/94, C:9/95.
2.2.4 Reduce manufacturing/distribution costs by 12% and response/delivery time by 5%: Mgt. Operations; B:12/93; S:6/94; C:9/95.
2.3.1 Implement a new quality control organization structure eliminating 2 layers of management by shifting responsibility for quality to shop floor operators: Mgr. Quality Control: B:12/93, S:9/94, C:3/95.

STRATEGIES

3.1 Improve participation and productivity.
3.2 Provide training to enhance opportunity.
3.3 Improve communications and strengthen loyalty.

TACTICS & ACCOUNTABILITY

3.1.2 Design employee involvement program to address cost and quality issues; achieve voluntary participation goals of: B:7/93
• 40% of emp. participating by 3/94
• 60% of emp. participating by 9/94
Director of Human Resources.
3.2.1 Establish specific training and development programs for all people: B:9/93
• > 80% of hourly employees by 3/94
• > 80% of management by 6/94
Director of Human Resources.
3.3.2 Institute weekly supervisory reports based on brief meetings to encourage employee communication of key concerns: Ops. Mgr.; B:9/93 — 85% supervisory compliance by 9/95.

STRATEGIES

4.1 Achieve financial benchmarks relative to competitors.
4.2 Achieve revenue growth goal at a targeted selling price/unit.
4.3 Achieve total commitment and active participation in planning process.

TACTICS & ACCOUNTABILITY

4.1.2 Attain return on equity of 16% or better (Top quartile of industry): GM: B:6/93, S:Quarterly, C:Yearly.
4.2.2 Achieve CAGR in revenues of 7% or more: GM Mktg. & Sales: B:6/93, S:Quarterly, C:Yearly.
4.4.3 Implement strategic control of plan implementation through quarterly reviews by Strategic Planning Council. Meet quarterly: VP Corp. Planning; C:3/94, quarterly thereafter.

Note:
B: Begin
S: Status Check
C: Complete

Figure 10-3. ABC Corporation—vision statement and strategic plan (schematic).

125

ABC CORPORATION
EXECUTIVE SHORT LIST

Short-Term Priorities

1.1.1 Install new sales/marketing organizational structure along product lines yet maintain expenses at current 10% of G&A.

1.2.1 Meet sales targets.

2.3.1 Eliminate two layers of management in quality control department by shifting quality responsibility to shop floor managers.

3.3.1 Establish specific training and development programs for all people.

4.3.1 Construct department plans showing at least a 2 to 4 percent cost reduction.

Long-Term Priorities

1.3.1 Identify growth opportunities in aircraft and/or transportation through effective market research.

2.1.3 Administer customer opinion surveys to attract a 15 to 20 percent response rate.

3.2.3 Design employee involvement program, with their participation, on quality and cost issues.

4.1.2 Attain return on operating equity of 16 percent or better by 1993.

4.2.2 Achieve CAGR of 7 percent or more in revenues over planning horizon.

Figure 10-4.

market share globally. The whole product line has been reengineered not once, but on a continual basis. When OMC managers focused on labor costs, they saw that their manufacturing operations were in large, difficult-to-manage plants in the northern United States. Their labor force has since been relocated to nine smaller non-union facilities in the southern United States, plus special purpose plants in Mexico, Hong Kong, and Brussels. OMC's labor cost, in adjusted dollars, is now less than half the hourly cost of 1980—and less than their Japanese competitors.

Strang's continuing focus on marine products later led to the sale of unrelated businesses such as Lawn Boy and Cushman, which manufac-

ABC CORPORATION
KEY OPERATING VOLUMES AND FINANCIAL GOALS

($ Millions)	1991	1992	Current Year 1993	Avg. Annual Growth (Comp'd) % 1988–1993 (E)	1994	1995	Plan 1996	1997	1998	Avg. Annual Growth (Comp'd) % 1993–1998
Sales (000's units)										
General Aviation	1285	1480	1398	1.9	1450	1510	1525	1545	1570	2.0
Target Markets	365	425	580	6.4	685	710	780	805	850	6.6
General Industrial	48	88	120	7.0	145	160	184	190	195	8.4
GSA	26	40	56	7.3	61	80	92	94	98	9.8
Net Sales	1300	1490	1326	6.9	1350	1480	1620	1875	2077	7.8
Gross Operating Profit	150	179	148	9.0	155	222	324	431	540	24.0
Net Operating Profit	40	61	42	(3.4)	51	78	92	114	141	22.4
Return on Sales, %	3.1	4.1	3.2	(9.6)	3.8	5.2	5.7	6.1	6.8	13.4
Average Equity	526	772	600	0.2	629	796	742	814	881	6.6
Return on Equity, %	7.6	7.9	7.0	(3.6)	8.1	9.8	12.4	14.0	16.0	14.8
Annual Depreciation	32	46	30	(12.9)	31	46	48	52	55	10.6
Capital Spending/Budget	47	78	36	(16.6)	40	120	15	20	10	(19.2)
Cash Generated/(Used)	10	(5)	15	(20.4)	20	(6)	120	128	136	44.4

Figure 10-5.

tured products for the lawn and garden industry. OMC has also acquired over 10 individual boat lines that utilize its engines. Today, OMC is strictly in the marine business. The focus represented by the three-page summary was only a reflection of the management focus in all aspects of Strang's strategy.

Rx for Leaders No. 6   Focus. Focus. Focus. Focus in your vision. Focus in your plan. Focus in your communications and operations.

Confidentiality

At some point in the third conference (if not earlier), as communication of the vision and plan to others is discussed, the question of confidentiality will be raised. It is a serious question. Generally, the leadership group feels quite comfortable talking about their mission, values, and long-term goals to almost any internal or external audience. But should strategies and tactics be kept under wraps?

Bob James, former vice president of product marketing and support for NCR, says, "We do not feel we need to keep our strategies a secret. In fact, we present them routinely to a variety of audiences, and require nothing in the way of confidentiality, or nondisclosure agreements. Basically, these strategies are available to all of our competitors, and we are relying on execution as a means to achieve competitive advantage, and create value for our customers."[7] Execution includes the tactics and accompanying accountability statements we outlined earlier. Tactics represent investments in human, physical, and other resources that are key to competitive advantage. They are generally not shared outside the top management group and are available on a need-to-know basis in the middle management group.

James goes on to say that "The by-product of having strategies that can be clearly articulated in public is that our customers know what to expect, they can better understand why we are doing certain things, and all employees receive a constant flow of information about our strategic fundamentals."[8] Many companies would not share NCR's openness with their strategies. This is an area that requires company-by-company decisions.

---

[7]"Airing Corporate Strategies," *Management Briefing: Marketing,* The Conference Board, February-March, 1989, with permission.

[8]Ibid.

In summary, the vision itself must be communicated openly, clearly, and repeatedly to all critical audiences, inside or outside the company, or understanding and implementation will be severely impeded. James makes an effective case for articulating strategies openly. Others feel just as strongly that their strategies need to remain proprietary. Specific tactics are considered proprietary by almost everybody.

Rx for Leaders No. 7   Communicate openly, clearly, and repeatedly. But remember, there are generally some things that must be kept confidential.

11

Communicating the Global Vision

The Long-Term Roll-Out

Father Theodore Hesburgh is a former president of the University of Notre Dame and served as the chief architect of Notre Dame's aspiration to be a leading university. His thoughts on the role of vision are very clear. "The very essence of leadership is you have to have a vision. It's got to be a vision you articulate clearly and forcibly on every occasion. You can't blow an uncertain trumpet."[1] This chapter provides trumpet lessons.

A number of roll-out activities are long-term in nature. These activities deal with communicating the vision to all key constituencies. To build a really great corporation "takes endless articulation and reinforcement of *what the institution honors, values, and believes.*"[2]

All the tasks described in the previous chapter can be completed in the third meeting or shortly thereafter. The development of the long-term roll-out program will include tasks generally initiated after the third meeting and before the first vision renewal meeting (which should occur approximately a year later). Suggested roll-out activities and examples will be outlined in this chapter by individual constituencies.

---

[1]"His Trumpet Was Never Uncertain," *Time*, May 18, 1987, p. 68.

[2]Richard T. Pascale and Anthony G. Athos, *The Art of Japanese Management*, Simon & Schuster, New York, 1981, pp. 170–171.

Rx for Leaders No. 1   Consider the options available in the long-term plan roll-out. The smart companies tend to use them all and then create a few of their own to match their personality.

The following are some suggested roll-out activities you can use with your corporate staff, your customers, your board of directors, and your shareholders and investors, as well as the community.

Your People

1. *Develop professionally printed copies of the corporate vision statement.* Bill Ruckelshaus at BFI wanted to tell his people and customers all over the world that he felt the BFI vision was something special. Figure 11-1 shows the summary he used. It was handsomely printed on recycled paper with careful attention to appearance and impact. The format itself said "special." For the global company, translation into the language of every area of operations will be required.

"Effective employee communications programs are pivotal to successful business strategies. That's something Federal Express has known for quite some time. In fact, it was founded on a philosophy based on People, Service, and Profit....Employee communications makes sure employees know what's going on, what's expected of them."[3]

2. *Create a series of short articles on the corporate vision statement written by the CEO.* Ruckelshaus elaborated on the BFI Vision with a series of one-page articles on the mission, values, and goals, which appeared in *The Blue Line*, the BFI internal newsletter (see Fig. 11-2). Pete Silas, Phillips Petroleum's CEO, prepared a two-page summary of the corporate vision and values for *PhilNews*, the internal Phillips newsletter (see Fig. 11-3).

3. *Produce a corporate video on the corporate vision statement.* To demonstrate the vision and values approach to business, Phillips produced a video of CEO Pete Silas presenting the vision statement, but Phillips did not stop there. The company was just completing a remarkble turnaround from the Pickens and Icahn takeover efforts and wanted to show examples of other turnaround companies rededicating themselves to future excellence. Phillips went to CEOs of other leading turnaround companies, including Don Peterson of Ford Motor Co. and Jack Reichert of Brunswick, and asked them to address their own vision and values and the contribution their cor-

---

[3]"FedEX Communicates, Then Communicates Some More," *Human Resources Briefing,* Volume 6, Number 7, The Conference Board, New York, September, 1990.

The Mission

Our mission is to provide the highest quality waste collection, transportation, processing, disposal and related services to both public and private customers worldwide. We will carry out our mission efficiently, safely and in an environmentally responsible manner with respect for the rule of government in protecting the public interest.

Our financial goal is to achieve consistently superior results that maintain BFI as a premier growth organization and maximize shareholder value.

The Foundation

BFI is built upon a solid foundation of sound operations, financial strength, and management depth and experience, but we must integrate our company further into the framework of our social, political and regulatory surroundings.

Values and Beliefs

We are dedicated to:

Our customers,
Our people,
The highest quality,
Continuous improvement,
Flexibility in the face of change,
Superior ethical conduct.

These are our values; these are what BFI stands for and what we believe to be the tools to accomplish the mission to which we are committed.

Our Goals

In our strategic planning for the decade ahead, we have reduced our goals to five specific areas. Each is supported by several strategies to attain the goal and by priority tactics to act upon in concert with those strategies.

Goal I. Quality
Provide the highest quality service to our customers so as to guarantee their satisfaction.

Goal II. Growth
Assure long-term growth and increase market share.

Goal III. People
Ensure that BFI has the people necessary to carry out our mission.

Goal IV. Ethical Conduct
Manage our business in a manner consistent with the public interest.

Goal V. Financial
Achieve consistently superior results that maintain BFI as a premier growth organization and maximize shareholder value.

With this Corporate Vision of the future, BFI is committed to these five goals.

Figure 11-1. Browning-Ferris mission for the 1990s.

BROWNING-FERRIS INDUSTRIES   JANUARY 1990

WILLIAM D. RUCKELSHAUS

COMMENTARY

Part of the Strategic Plan which BFI has recently adopted to help guide our future is a section entitled *Values and Beliefs*. We felt it necessary to probe deeply into what was important to the people of BFI – what principles had guided our growth and our conduct over the last twenty years. We asked many in the company to help us formulate this fundamental underpinning and we finally sifted out those values and beliefs we felt were at the core of the people of BFI.

Now we all have values and beliefs. But I don't think very many of us write them down. After all, they are usually kind of personal, and since we live with

them every day, there is no need to write them down. Our strategic planning group did because we wanted to be sure that all of us at BFI now, or who will join us in the future, understand what we believe is fundamental to the success of the company. If we adhere to these values and beliefs, if we manage the company consistent with their promise, we will stay on the road toward greatness.

In no particular order, because they are all equally important, you, the employees of BFI, told us your values and beliefs were as follows: "We are dedicated to our customers, our people, the highest quality, continuous improvement, flexibility in the face of change and ethical conduct."

There they are: our customers, our people, quality, continuous improvement, flexibility and ethical conduct. Are they equally important? The simple answer is yes. But every time you lay them out, ethical conduct kind of shoulders its way to the front. We can be dedicated to our customers and to each other as employees, but if we don't practice the highest ethical standards, our dedication would sound a little hollow. We are certainly dedicated to continuous improvement, to the highest quality, and where the only constant is change, we know we have to stay flexible just to survive. But if we take our eye off the superior ethical conduct ball, no amount of talk about quality, flexibility or improvement is going to ring true, either with each other, with our customers or those governmental entities we must satisfy and serve.

In the past, a very few BFI employees failed the superior ethical conduct test. It is tossed back at us still, sometimes years later, by those who are opposed to what we are trying to do, like open a landfill, or who simply want to shine a bright light on us before giving us a contract or their business. And they should shine the light. With our values and beliefs intact, we'll shine back just as brightly as their light.

Okay, what is "superior ethical conduct" exactly? In my view, it is being able to put what you say and what you do on a billboard alongside of the highway you travel to work every day ... along with your friends, family, co-workers and customers ... and not be ashamed.

Sure the laws a company like BFI has to comply with are complex. From antitrust to detailed, unclear, even baffling regulations regarding the operation of our landfills, it is not easy to never be accused. But we must not hide behind ignorance of the law. Fundamentally, we all know what amounts to ethical conduct – what is right and what isn't. Superior ethical conduct is simply doing what's right ... whether anyone is looking or not.

We have said now, publicly, that one of our values and beliefs is superior ethical conduct. That's not just some of us ... that is the whole company, all 25,400 of us, all over the world where the BFI sign is. BFI STANDS FOR SUPERIOR ETHICAL CONDUCT! That's the way we treat our customers. That's the way we treat each other. That's the way we treat everyone with whom we come in contact. It is one of our values and beliefs.

Are we perfect? Nope. Are we aiming too high? Absolutely not. We are aiming for success in our business. And we aim to be successful by being ethical.

Figure 11-2. *Blue Line* commentary.

Between Us

By Pete Silas
Chairman and
Chief Executive Officer

Where We're Going ...

Earlier this year, we gathered together a group of key people from all parts of our company for an important assignment. We asked this diverse group to try to define three things — as simply and as clearly as possible:

1. What is Phillips Petroleum Company?
2. What do we want to accomplish as a company?
3. And what principles should guide us as we pursue our business objectives?

To some, the answers to these questions might seem obvious and not something that would require a lot of discussion. But as it turned out, the answers weren't so easy to come up with. There was disagreement on many points and a lot of lively discussion within the group. And it became very clear that in view of all the changes that have taken place in our industry and in our company in recent years, it would be a good idea to reaffirm for all employees just who we are, what we believe in and what we're trying to accomplish.

As a result, we plan to give strong emphasis in the months ahead to what we call our corporate "mission," a statement that defines our company and establishes our key objectives. We plan to give equally strong emphasis to our company's "values and beliefs," a set of statements that puts on record the guiding principles that have contributed significantly over the years to our company's success.

Figure 11-3. *PhilNews* 1988.

What we are ...

An integrated petroleum company that explores for, produces and upgrades oil and natural gas into petroleum products and chemicals for our customers.

Defining ourselves ...

When most people think of Phillips Petroleum Company, they think of our Phillips 66 shield and our service stations. Inside the company, we know that Phillips is involved in much more than selling gasoline and other products to motorists. We find and produce crude oil and natural gas. We operate refineries and chemical plants and engage in dozens of other business activities. However, most of these activities are related. Phillips is what our industry calls an "integrated" company. This means that our operations fit together, reinforcing each other and giving us the potential to generate more value as an overall unit than the separate parts could generate by themselves. We consider this integration our company's most important strength, and our plans for the future will be oriented toward finding new ways to make the most of this advantage.

Our mission is ...

To enhance the value of our shareholders' investment by using the strengths of our people and our integrated operations to provide our customers with products that are high in quality and competitive in price.

Generating value ...

There are important reasons why our company mission is oriented toward our shareholders. Those who own our stock are the real "owners" of Phillips — people who have chosen to invest in our company instead of using their money in some other way. Our job is to make sure that our shareholders receive a competitive return on their investment, both through dividends and through increases in the price of our stock. This emphasis on shareholders doesn't mean we can afford to neglect others who have a stake in our company's success. Clearly, we can't expect to deliver satisfactory performance for shareholders on a sustained basis unless we continue to give good treatment to our customers and the people who work for our company. And this means continuing to improve our businesses and to carry out research for the future. (See our key objectives below.) We're also encouraging Phillips people to become shareholders and to increase their ownership of the company through additional stock purchases. The more stock we own, the more we're working directly for our own benefit. Through our new Long-Term Stock Savings Plan, employees can vote more than 20 percent of the company's stock, one of the highest percentages of any publicly traded company.

How do we measure success?

Setting a goal is only part of the job. We have to figure out ways to attain the goal and track our progress to make sure we're moving in the right direction. So in order to measure our progress toward accomplishing our mission, we've established corporate objectives. Our key objective is to provide a competitive shareholder return (price appreciation plus dividends) in the top 25 percent of the industry group.

Here's where we stand:

Enhancing Investment Value
Total Return (includes stock appreciation & dividends)

Here's how much a $100 investment in one of these stocks would have grown ...	So far this year 1/1/88-9/30/88	After one year 9/30/87-9/30/88
Phillips	$139	$121
Unocal	128	94
Sun	117	100
Arco	116	86
Amerada Hess	114	82
Occidental	113	82
Amoco	111	95
7-Co. Average	$120	$94

Our other corporate objectives:

- Generate an operating return on assets in each of our core businesses which ranks in the top 25 percent of the industry.
- Attain an investment-grade rating on our debt by:
  — reducing debt to $4.5 billion by 1990;
  — increasing equity to $3 billion by 1991.
- Operate each of our businesses in an efficient, low-cost, high-quality manner, maintaining high standards of ethics, safety and environmental compliance.

- Provide access to technology and utilize that technology to improve the competitive position of each of our businesses.
- Build employee commitment, pride and loyalty and provide challenging opportunities in a continuously changing environment.
- Enhance customer relationships through high-quality products and services.

We believe in ...

- **Treating one another with respect.**
- **Giving equal opportunity to every employee.**
- **Maintaining a safe work environment.**
- **Conducting ourselves ethically and responsibly.**
- **Communicating openly and honestly.**
- **Supporting individual creativity and innovation.**
- **Providing our customers with top-quality products and services.**
- **Protecting the environment.**
- **Contributing to the quality of life wherever we operate.**

Our values ...

Our company mission and our corporate objectives tell us **what** we're trying to accomplish. Our beliefs and values give us boundary lines in the pursuit of those accomplishments. In other words, we're committing ourselves to stay within the boundaries even if there appears to be some short-term advantage to violating one of our principles. As human beings, we all make mistakes. And there have been times when we've failed to live up to some of the beliefs listed here. Realistically, we know that this may happen in the future. But let's all make a sincere effort to observe these values and beliefs. And if and when some company action seems out of step with these specific principles, let's work together to bring it to light and try to make sure it doesn't happen again.

Figure 11-3. (*Continued*)

porate vision statement had made in regaining industry leadership. Phillips then incorporated their responses into the video.

Videos like this can be multipurpose vehicles for the company. They are excellent tools in employee orientation, recruiting, management, and employee development. They are also of assistance in acquisition negotiations to portray the personality and culture of the organization.

BFI took the video idea a step further. Taped portions of the third LCPP meeting were combined with informal commentaries by its principal officers, along with some earlier footage of key corporate events. The composite provided an excellent half-hour history of BFI's corporate accomplishments over the last 20 years. The tape is used extensively for all the purposes mentioned above.

4. *Conduct small discussion groups.* Written communication and video presentations can never take the place of one-on-one contacts. These small group meetings, whether over lunch or in a discussion group, are the only way to respond to questions and secure feedback. The most successful organizations will always include this alternative in their roll-out plan. It is even more important in the global company where there are some very real language and cultural barriers. The leader and the leadership group should include these discussions in the agenda of their global travels.

5. *Create laminated wallet-size corporate vision statement cards.* Many clients have taken the core mission statement, values, and goals and reproduced them on a laminated credit-card size card to be carried in a wallet. Other clients have laminated the vision statement on ID cards, frequently carried as a pocket clip-on. (See Chap. 5, Fig. 5-1, for an example from Motorola).

Rx for Leaders No. 2   Send a message to your people that the corporate vision is something special by having it professionally printed and by writing a series of articles elaborating on the company's mission, values, and goals. When the CEO spends his or her own time on something, people know it is important.

Rx for Leaders No. 3   Use a video to communicate your vision statements. It's the next best thing to sitting down with every employee on an individual basis. If you are a global company with thousands of employees, there is probably no other way to get to everybody.

Rx for Leaders No. 4   Include small-group discussions wherever you or your leadership group go; they are essential to every roll-out program. If you really want to improve a company's culture, this is a must. Not once, but repetitively.

Your Customers

6. Use the corporate vision statement as a theme for an executive call on a major customer (particularly those you have had consistent difficulties with) or a major prospect (particularly those you just can't close). It may provide a new foundation on which you can build. If it does not already exist, institute a customer or client feedback mechanism to link with your Total Quality Program.

7. Send a copy of the corporate vision statement to all your customers. The vision statement can be an excellent means of communicating corporate culture or personality to customers.

Rx for Leaders No. 5   Make sure your major customers and prospects recognize that your corporate vision and total quality program are tightly linked. One cannot succeed without the other.

Rx for Leaders No. 6   Send a copy of your completed vision statement, especially your corporate values, to all your customers. Then make sure your warranty and customer service programs back them up.

Your Board of Directors

8. Use the corporate vision statement and strategic plan to justify or sell major programs. Charlie Strang and Jim Chapman did this beautifully at Outboard Marine Corporation in justifying a $100 million manufacturing relocation program from the northern to southern United States. The projected labor cost reduction and internal rate of return on the move was attractive, but there was also a lot of risk. The ultimate selling point for the board of directors was neither the labor cost reduction or the internal rate of return, but OMC's survival as the world leader in outboard engines.

9. Base the incentive compensation program on the corporate vision and supporting strategic plan. Strang sealed his agreement with the Board by proposing that the incentive compensation plan for himself and the core group be based on the same market share and profit goals that were included in their strategic plan supporting their global vision.

Rx for Leaders No. 7   Sell your large capital programs based on your vision. Cost reduction and the internal rate of return can sell smaller programs, but not your major investments.

Rx for Leaders No. 8   Base your incentive compensation plan on your corporate vision and link them tightly. Your board of directors and top management will take your corporate vision and supporting strategic plan more seriously.

Your Shareholders and Investors

10. *Build your annual report around the theme of the corporate vision statement.* For the shareholder this is an even more effective means of communicating than a special publication. It stands the best chance of being read and also shows how the vision and strategic plan are incorporated into day-to-day operations. GE and IBM have done this very effectively.

11. *Use your vision as the theme for analyst presentations.* Many of the analysts say they are interested only in the numbers. If you give them just what they want, they will never understand what you are trying to do (mission and goals) and what you intend to emphasize as you try to get it done (values). Using the vision and values approach allows them to see the numbers in context. I want to emphasize again that vision and values do not substitute for performance. They must be seen as the motivating force behind performance.

Rx for Leaders No. 9   Convince analysts that the vision and values are the ultimate keys to market performance. Make sure they understand that connection.

Community and Regulatory Bodies

12. *Use the vision-related articles and video to enhance community and regulatory relations.* By the time you engage one of these bodies you are often in a

request or confrontational mode. You want a zoning variance or have an environmental problem. Take the time to make sure they know who you are and what you stand for. Help them see your vision for your company and your people, and use your video and related articles. They may have the same uplifting effect on regulatory bodies that they had on your leadership group and your people. They certainly are not confrontational, and may help some people to see you in a more positive light.

Orientation and Repetition

Vision and values are particularly important to companies in periods of rapid growth, like Progressive, a new billion-dollar property and casualty insurance company in Mayfield, Ohio: "Hiring employees by the thousand and inoculating them with the corporate mission is a huge challenge. At Progressive, which doubled its work force with 2600 new hires in 1986 and 1987, a training program drums in watchwords like integrity, aspiration, excellence, respect for all people, and profit. Says chairman Lewis: `We make a constant effort to reward people who understand our values and objectives, and to cull those who do not.'"[4]

Repetition is one of the keys to communication and commitment. The roll-out activities discussed previously represent mechanisms for a repetition of the corporate vision statement. The corporate vision "must be repeated time and again. It must be incorporated in the organization's culture and reinforced through the strategy and decision-making process....Another way the leader communicates a new vision is by consistently acting on it and personifying it."[5]

Walk Your Talk

People are very receptive to a new vision statement, although they seem to take a wait-and-see attitude to validate their first impression. If they see the leader or leaders acting in line with their stated vision, they will begin to do the same, although perhaps a little more slowly than we would like. The pace usually quickens as the leaders continue to live out their stated beliefs.

But if the people detect that their leaders' actions are different from their words, the whole exercise can backfire. It is not the vision that

---

[4]William E. Sheeline, "Avoiding Growth's Perils," *Fortune*, August 13, 1990, p. 58, with permission.

[5]Warren Bennis and Burt Nanus, *Leaders: The Strategies for Taking Charge*, HarperCollins Publishers Inc., New York, 1985, pp. 108 and 109.

backfires, but subsequent action that people see as conflicting with the vision. It is the difference between the politician's campaign speech and what is done in office. The leaders must walk their talk. Failures may occur, but their actions must consistently concur with the vision on an overall basis.

Global Values Require an Open Mind

More than openness is required in search of global values. Managers and people in the EC, Far East, Russia, and the emerging market economies of Eastern Europe each have a set of values, although the values may never have been made explicit before. The ideal is to actively search out those values in a participative format much like that described in the Leadership Conference Planning Process.

Different countries or regions will have some difficulty regarding true ownership of corporate values that have come from a totally different culture. However, they can develop a strong sense of ownership of values arising from their own culture that will give them the same sense of inner drive and motivation.

> **Rx for Leaders No. 10**   Values are meant to stir the heart, not close the mind. Be open to additional values of particular importance to a geographic area or business unit.

The CEO's Roll-Out Check List

A CEO check list for a successful roll-out is summarized in Fig. 11-4.

THE CEO'S ROLL-OUT CHECK LIST

- Your vision is crisp and concise. Make certain the strategies, tactics, etc., are concluded quickly with the same discipline and care.

- Make certain that the task force leaders are and remain the champions of their respective goals. Their job is just beginning.

- The task force leaders should participate with you in the presentation of the plan to all your people. It is an important presentation, and rehearsal is a must.

- Prepare your Executive Short List (long-term and short-term goals) based on what you want your people and your board to focus on particularly.

- Get personally involved with the assumptions and expected results contained in your financial summary. Make your assumptions explicit for yourself and the board.

- Develop professionally printed versions of the corporate vision statement for broad distribution.

- Write a short article for the company's newsletter on your own views of each element of the corporate vision statement. Jot down some notes now while it's fresh in your mind.

- Consider a video of the plan presentation for your people, new hires, training, etc.

- Establish some small discussion groups for direct feedback and to achieve a higher level of commitment.

- Consider use of the corporate vision statement theme in key customer calls or presentations. Ask the customer to tell you when and where you don't live up to it.

- Use the corporate vision statement to sell your board on major programs. Try to establish it as the basis for compensation.

Figure 11-4.

12
Making the Vision a Reality

Stewardship

Timely and consistent stewardship is critical to making your vision a reality and to renewing the vision so that it retains vitality. At the end of the third (or commitment) conference of The Leadership Conference Planning Process (LCPP), there is generally a "high" among core group members. They feel they have accomplished something significant in the life of the corporation. There is also a sigh of relief that they are over the hump and the hard work is completed. But, in fact, it isn't; it has just begun. As we mentioned earlier, it generally takes 3 years to get a corporate vision and strategic plan process wired in to the organization. By "wired in" I mean that management looks upon the vision and strategic plan as the consistent guidance system for the future, as well as a check point for any new ventures or major initiatives.

"Fragmentation, the loss of shared values, and the difficulty of reconciling antagonistic forces are not the only organizational problems the leader must deal with today. Leaders discover that the great systems over which they preside require continuous renewal....Motivation tends to run down. Values decay. The problems of today go unsolved....But the cycle of birth, maturity, and death is not inexorable in organizations and societies as it is in living things. Renewal is possible."[1] In fact, renewal is essential; small vision-renewal events are needed several times a year and a larger renewal event annually. This

[1] Reprinted with the permission of The Free Press, a division of Macmillan, Inc. *On Leadership* by John W. Gardner, p. 121. Copyright © 1990 by John W. Gardner.

chapter and the next will review a recommended structure for those events in some detail.

Without renewal, leaders themselves can become obstacles to a vision in time. Internal management controls and accountability systems cannot address this problem. When leaders become obstacles, the shareholders through the board of directors must discharge their responsibility to bring in new leadership. RCA had to change leaders three times in 10 years, and the company still ended up being acquired by GE. GM's leaders had a near-crisis recently, IBM has one now, and there will be others. If management does not renew itself, the board must.

In order to survive, a leader must make *service* the goal. As one CEO states, "The goal of renewal is to be a corporate entity that gives us space to reach our potential as individuals and, through that, as a corporation. Renewal comes through genuine service to others. It cannot come about through a process of mere self-perpetuation. Renewal is an outward orientation of service, rather than an inward orientation of maintenance. Renewal is the concern of everyone."[2] Self-perpetuation will be recognized by the board and the people in the organization. Both will look for genuine service. If they fail to find it, they may not say anything until it is too late for the leader to launch a renewal initiative.

Rx for Leaders No. 1   Make service your goal and not self-perpetuation. It is not uncommon for leaders to become the obstacles. Don't let it happen to you.

Strategic Vital Signs

Some clearly identified vital signs can help gauge the health of the corporate vision. Benjamin Tregoe, John Zimmerman, Ronald Smith, and Peter Tobia, in *Vision in Action,* constructed a list that is worthy of reflection.

- **A common strategic reference point:** *"Is there a common strategic reference point down through the organization?"*[3] Sharing in the development of the corporate vision and strategic plan should certainly provide the common strategic reference point for the leaders in the core group. Chapters 10 and 11, which discuss communicating the vision, focus on

---

[2]Max DePree, *Leadership Is an Art,* Doubleday, New York, 1989, p. 80, with permission.

[3]Benjamin B. Tregoe, John W. Zimmerman, Ronald A. Smith, and Peter M. Tobia, *Vision in Action: Putting a Winning Strategy to Work,* Simon & Schuster, New York, 1989, p. 104. Copyright © 1989 by Kepner-Tregoe, Inc., with permission.

achieving ownership of the vision throughout the organization.

- **Aligning structure with vision:** *"Have the implications of vision for the formal and informal organizational structure been addressed?"*[4] The leader and the core group addressed this point in the business segmentation discussion as part of the overall corporate mission. Chapter 3 pointed out that this segmentation should follow the current corporate organization. But sometimes it doesn't, and there can be serious misalignment. Changing the structure and then keeping it aligned with the strategy reaches the highest level of strategy implementation.

- **Relating culture and vision:** *"Is there consistency between the organization's culture and vision?"*[5] The leader and the core group have looked at the corporate mission, values, and goals in the same time frame and in the same context in the three leadership conferences (see Chaps. 7 to 9). That is probably the best insurance of consistency that can be offered.

These first three "vital signs of vision" have been addressed in the earlier chapters of this book. The rest of this chapter presents the last three vital signs addressed by Tregoe, Zimmerman, Smith, and Tobia:

- **Monitoring vision's success:** *"Are monitoring systems to track and measure strategic effectiveness in place?"* (See the quarterly plan reviews that follow.)

- **Critical issues management:** *"Are critical strategic issues continually identified and resolved?"* (See the quarterly plan reviews that follow.)

- **Keeping vision current:** *"Have periodic reviews and updates of the vision been provided for?"*[6] (See the description of the annual renewal process in this chapter.)

The longer-term tasks of the leader and the core group are establishing effective quarterly reviews of the strategic plan, as well as instituting an annual renewal process that moves the organization toward making their vision a reality on a timely basis. These two processes, the quarterly plan reviews and the annual renewal, must continue indefinitely.

Rx for Leaders No. 2   Put accountability and renewal on the list of things that go on forever. It can be interesting and rewarding to make an important sales call or solve a manufacturing problem. Establishing accountability and renewal are more important. And they are your job.

---

[4]Ibid.

[5]Ibid.

[6]Ibid.

Quarterly Plan Reviews

Quarterly reviews are generally a half to three-quarters of a day in length, depending on the level of detail the CEO requires in progress reporting. They should never last longer than a day unless they are linked with the annual revision of the strategic plan, which will be addressed later in this chapter. The meetings should be attended by all members of the original core group. Ideally, scheduling of the quarterly reviews should be in line with the already established internal business calendar, and should be scheduled 1 or 2 weeks prior to the quarterly board meeting. This allows the quarterly review to serve as a meaningful strategy update for the CEO and any other internal board members.

The quarterly plan reviews must address several objectives:

- *Keep appropriate levels of management informed of plan progress:* At a minimum, the quarterly plan reviews must be attended by the task force leaders, the CEO, and the meld group. At a maximum, they will include all members of the core group and other managers on an as-needed basis.

- *Demonstrate plan visibility and accountability:* I mentioned in the last chapter that managers outside the core group, as well as most employees, do not automatically commit to the new vision and strategic plan. Instead, they wait for evidence that it is not going to take a quick trip to the corporate boneyard. The *quarterly reviews* are continuing evidence of management's accountability and serious intent regarding implementation.

- *Provide a forum to discuss key corporate strategic opportunities and threats:* There must be a regularly available forum for these discussions. At times, these discussions will lead to specific new tactics to address the opportunity or threat. At other times, further formal or informal discussion will be required. The critical point is to provide an open and timely forum for the discussions.

- *Adopt timely corrective action to address changes in the company's internal or external environment:* The strategic plan and supporting tactics can only be as current as the date the plan was completed. I suggest that overall plan revisions be done on an annual basis only, so that the plan has some stability. It is important, however, that new tactics or action plans be developed to address changes in the customer, as well as in the competitive and economic environment. The same characteristics that applied to the original plan tactics should apply to these tactics: brief, action oriented, quantitative, and specific, with a clear delegation of responsibility.

■ *Integrate plan operating and financial performance:* Some corporations feel it is essential to discuss financial performance in both an operating and a strategic mode. I agree. The quarterly plan review provides the opportunity to discuss the long-term implications of financial performance, as opposed to the more normal operating implications.

Rx for Leaders No. 3   Use the quarterly reviews to assure your people of strong accountability. They are naturally cautious about new visions, and will wait for evidence that the vision is not going to take a quick trip to the corporate boneyard before they begin to commit to it.

Quarterly Review Agenda

The quarterly review agenda focuses on two major subjects—*tactical accountability* and *key corporate issues.* These two broad agenda items are appropriate for any organization:

■ **Tactical Accountability:** A progress check on strategic plan tactics and demonstration of accountability.

■ **Key Corporate Issues:** An open discussion of strategic opportunities, threats, and environmental issues, and the adoption of appropriate action.

Another potential subject is quarterly financial performance in those organizations that feel it is helpful or necessary to look at financial performance from a strategic perspective.

The scheduled time should be fairly evenly split between the two major topics. The tactical accountability portion of the agenda should address Tregoe's fourth vital sign, with monitoring systems to track strategic effectiveness already in place. Each tactic is the responsibility of a given individual. If more than one person is listed as responsible for the tactic, the first person listed should have primary responsibility for it.

The task force leader for each goal defined in the leadership conferences is generally called the goal executive, or manager, after plan development is completed. The goal manager is responsible for knowing the status of each tactic included under the goal and for reporting on tactic status at the quarterly review if the person with prime responsibility is not at the meeting. The goal manager effectively becomes the continuing goal champion.

The report on each tactic scheduled for review or completion should be succinct and definitive. It is not necessary for reports to be formal. Handouts or simple overhead transparencies are preferred.

- No report is required when the tactic has not yet reached its scheduled completion date unless there is a need to revise the completion date or to change or delete the tactic.

- When a completion date has been reached, and the tactic has been completed, the person responsible for tactic completion (or the goal champion) should make a concise report of results, with a recommendation to release the tactic from further reporting subject to the CEO's concurrence.

- When a completion date has been reached but the tactic has not been completed, the person responsible for tactic completion (or the goal champion) should give a clear definition of any change requested in terms of tactic content or direction (including the specific wording suggested) or in the scheduled completion date.

- When an interim milestone date has been reached:

  A status report is due.

  The person responsible for tactic completion (or the goal champion) should give a clear definition of any change requested in terms of tactic content or direction (the specific wording suggested) or in the next review or completion date.

- The status of all items on the "Executive Short List" (see Chap. 10, Fig. 10-4) should be reported at each review.

Some firms prepare a brief, written summary for each tactic that has reached a completion date for circulation before the meeting. The intent is to ensure that meeting time is spent only on those issues requiring group action or deliberation.

A discussion of strategic opportunities and threats follows. This portion of the agenda addresses Tregoe's fifth vital sign regarding continually identifying and resolving critical issues. It is the more proactive of the two topics and is the primary means of making the overall vision and strategic planning process a living process. The discussion of strategic issues is led by the CEO, who solicits input a month or so prior to the meeting. The major issues to be discussed are identified for all the attendees so that they can prepare themselves adequately. Close records of these critical issues should be maintained until the CEO feels they have been adequately addressed.

Group discussion of the opportunities and threats may lead to the development of new tactics and new accountabilities. In this sense, the strategic plan is a living document or "evergreen," as opposed to something that comes alive only once a year when it is completely revised.

Although the monitoring of tactical progress on original or new tactics does have the flavor of an audit, it is essential for demonstrating accountability. And accountability is essential to ensure strategic progress over time in any organization of any size. "Some who exercise power can be trusted to be adequately self-critical and disciplined, but it is a poor assumption on which to base…policy. The simple rule is: *Hold power accountable.*"[7] In the final analysis, the vision and the strategic plan that the leader and the core group have put together will become the vehicle to "hold power accountable." It is extremely effective in this regard, because the leader and the core group created the document in the first place, on a highly participative basis. If those people are not measured and held accountable, an awful lot of things just don't get done. Remember David Packard's comment in Chap. 7, "Tell me how you are going to measure me, and I'll tell you how I'll act."[8] The quarterly reviews are the key to measurement and accountability.

> **Rx for Leaders No. 4**   Monitor plan progress on a regular basis. Things don't get done unless people are held accountable.

> **Rx for Leaders No. 5**   Discuss and resolve critical business issues on a timely basis. Do it in the context of the corporate vision and supporting strategic plan.

The Annual Renewal Process: Making the Vision a Reality

The annual renewal process should be the principal time for management renewal of the fundamental vision and values of the organization. The other items on the agenda are concerned with the implementation of the vision.

---

[7]Gardner, p. 153.

[8]David Packard, *Harvard Business Review*, November-December, 1988, p. 194.

In an unchanging world, the corporate vision and strategic plan would never have to be revisited. The basic culprits that create the need for periodic renewal are the natural disintegration of vision and values without nurturing and the rate of change in the external business environment. The vast majority of organizations with a well-established strategic planning process revise their plans on an annual basis. Corporate vision must also be revisited and the commitment to it renewed. The annual renewal fulfills a number of very important objectives:

- To achieve renewed consensus and commitment regarding the original vision.
- To consider and address changes in the business environment since initial plan formulation.
- To rewrite elements of the strategic plan requiring revision.

The timing of the annual vision and plan renewal is another consideration. It certainly should precede the budgetary process in the annual calendar and generally seems to work best if it does so by approximately 6 months. If the budgetary process occurs in the fall, I recommend the renewal process be held in the spring to allow a bit of time (and vacations) in between. Some companies like to schedule the renewal process so that it abuts the budgetary process. They will frequently schedule it for June through August, to be followed immediately by the budgetary process beginning in September. There are just two rules I would consider to be inviolable in timing the plan renewal:

- The budget process and the plan renewal should never be scheduled together. The short-term focus of one and the long-term focus of the other force the participants to choose between them, and it is generally the short-term budget process that wins out. It is more familiar, routine, and habitual.
- The renewal process should *always* precede the budgetary process in the calendar year.

Rx for Leaders No. 6   Keep budgets and strategy out of the same room. Budget is short-term. Strategy is long-term. If forced to choose, people will opt for the short term almost every time.

Meeting Structure

The annual renewal is attended by all members of the core group and generally is held in conjunction with the first and second quarterly reviews of the year. This will be explained under revision of the strategic plan. There are four general elements in the meeting structure:

- A review of the corporate vision
- A self-appraisal regarding progress made during the past year via a confidential questionnaire
- A special-focus item or items
- A revision of the supporting strategic plan

A Review of the Corporate Vision.   The corporate vision must be reviewed in some depth each year at the renewal session. All three elements of the corporate vision (values and beliefs, mission, and goals) have a long-time horizon. They should seldom be revised, and then for clarification only. But there are other aspects to this review. The principal one is to assess how well the leaders and the corporation are living out the vision. Even if no changes are made, and the core group is satisfied with it, the annual renewal process should be the principal time for management to recommit to the fundamental vision and values of the organization. The renewal process in action, particularly the review of the corporate vision, is the subject of Chapter 13

A Self-Appraisal.   Before the first LCPP meeting (discussed in Chap. 6), each member of the core group completed a confidential questionnaire. The responses constituted a group assessment of the strategic position and outlook of the organization. Before the first annual renewal meeting begins, another confidential questionnaire should be used to assess each member's opinion of the progress achieved in the past year, and their estimation of what is required in the coming years if the organization is to move toward its vision. A summary of the questionnaire results should be presented as one of the initial agenda items in the renewal meeting. It provides a source of both general and specific ideas to direct the organization's thinking and action. Figure 12-1 is an example of an annual renewal process questionnaire. It emphasizes progress, commitment, and accountability relative to the vision and strategic plan.

A Special Focus Item.   The purpose of the annual renewal process is to rekindle the vision, recommit the leadership group to it, and readapt the strategic plan to a changing environment. The process

---

ANNUAL RENEWAL PROCESS

CONFIDENTIAL QUESTIONNAIRE

1. It has been nearly one year since we completed our Corporate Vision and Strategic Plan. In your opinion, how are things going? Please circle your rating on the scale below, 20 being the highest.

   20 19 18 17 16 15 14 13 12 11 10 9 8 7 6 5 4 3 2 1

   Comments:

2. Are the vision and plan recognized as a part of our management system? Do our communications effectively support and reinforce their implementation?

3. Do we have adequate commitment and accountability?

4. Do you have specific changes to suggest in our values or mission?

5. Do you have specific changes to suggest in our long-term goals or strategies?

6. Have we made adequate progress toward plan implementation, i.e., tactics and accountability?

7. Are our product volume and financial goals challenging? Achievable?

8. What are the major challenges (either opportunities or problems) we face over the next 5–10 years? Does our plan address them adequately?

9. What do we need to do from a tactical point of view (in the next 12–24 months) to address these challenges?

Figure 12-1. Annual renewal process questionnaire.

should be stimulating and reenergizing; drudgery and routine are its enemies. While the purpose of the meeting is constant, its theme and focus must change each year. The focus one year might be total quality, with an outside speaker to provide a new or special light on the subject. Customer satisfaction or leadership are also good themes. The special focus item will be discussed at more length in the next chapter.

Rx for Leaders No. 7   Defeat routine and drudgery in the annual renewal process. Create a new focus each year, and change the theme and format.

A Revision of the Strategic Plan. The annual renewal process is generally built around the first and second quarterly reviews of the year. The first quarterly review is usually about a day and a half in length, and the second usually takes a day.

The first part of the first meeting should follow the format suggested for regular quarterly reviews. This ensures that the group as a whole first looks at progress to date on tactics included in the previous year's plan and then at the external environment and new issues, both opportunities as well as challenges, that may have arisen. The meeting also includes the review of the corporate vision and a special focus item (discussed earlier).

In the last part of the meeting, the goal champion for each goal should be asked to outline any changes in strategy as well as new or revised tactics that the task force expects to propose at the next meeting. This is generally followed by a discussion and some general suggestions and recommendations from the CEO and other members of the core group.

The goal champions reconvene their task force between the two quarterly reviews for a strategic and tactical update of their specific goal. The goal champions present their recommendations goal by goal in the day set aside for the second quarterly review and for final discussion by the core group and approval by the leader.

Rx for Leaders No. 8 Get direct, open, and honest feedback from your leadership group and expand your input beyond them. Your strategic performance record requires candid input, and the confidential questionnaire is the ticket.

Rx for Leaders No. 9 Keep your vision stable. Revision should be minor and infrequent. The annual review will allow you to calibrate your performance in achieving your vision and regain a sense of commitment to it.

Failures in Stewardship: "The Least Admired Companies"

In addition to its annual listing of "Most Admired Companies," *Fortune* also provides an annual listing of the "Least Admired Companies." Half the companies that have appeared on the list have appeared only one time. Several were as outstanding in their time as almost any of *Fortune*'s "Most Admired Companies." The list has included A&P, F. W. Woolworth, RCA, U.S. Steel, Union Carbide, and Manufacturer's Hanover Bank. The founders of each of these companies initially had a compelling vision and a set of values that powered them to positions of prominence. However, part of the long-term stewardship responsibility is the periodic renewal of the vision that was the basis of that early power. It was a failure in stewardship by the founders' successors that led to these corporations' downfall. There are few companies, if any, in which the founder was still CEO when the firm first appeared on the least admired list.

Certainly some of the companies were very much influenced by a difficult industry environment, such as the steel and metal industry. Companies that have appeared on the least admired list from the steel and metals industry include AMAX, Asarco, Bethlehem Steel, Kaiser Aluminum, LTV, National Steel, Republic Steel, and USX. But they cannot be excused for their failure in vision or values because of a poor industry business environment. Many of their competitors, such as Alcoa, Armco, Inland Steel, Nucor, Phelps Dodge and Reynolds Metals, never appeared on this list. If a company lands on this list, they generally deserve it.

As *Fortune* points out, "The least admired rarely stay in the cellar for more than a few years. The bad news is that many of them escape it by getting swallowed up. That fate in recent years claimed American Motors and Financial Corp. of America."[9] American Motors is a clear champion among the "Least Admired Companies." It appeared on the list in 1982, the first time the list was published, and stayed on it every year through 1987, when it was acquired by Chrysler. Texas Air also followed this escape route after appearing on the list for 3 years before being acquired by Continental in 1990. Now it appears on the list as Continental Airlines Holdings. Hardly a business analyst in the country doubts that the companies on this list earned their way.

A breakdown in basic values will also dim a corporate vision. This may be the underlying factor in the appearance of four savings and loans on the list in the past few years, including Financial Corporation of America, Gibraltar Financial, Meritor Financial, and Goldome. One of the recurring values in many of the "Most Admired Companies" is the relative lack of importance placed on their employees. It is not surprising that seven of the companies that have appeared on *Fortune*'s "Least Admired

---

[9]"Leaders of the Most Admired," *Fortune*, January 29, 1990, p. 63, with permission.

Companies" list also appear on the list of the Ten Biggest Pension Fund Deficits in the United States. If they don't value their people while they are on the payroll, why worry about them after they are retired?

> **Rx for Leaders No. 10**   Don't allow a failure in stewardship. These failures are not the fault of the new stewards alone. Fault also lies with the preceding leaders who put the stewards in place, and theirs may be the greater fault.

13

The Renewal Process in Action

Renewal and rekindling of the corporate vision and values are the subjects of this chapter. *"Values always decay over time. Societies that keep their values alive do so not by escaping the processes of decay but by powerful processes of regeneration.* There must be perpetual rebuilding....Only living values count. They must be reflected in actual behavior."[1]

Some say that "leaders are closer to the architect dealing with the problems of renovation than they are to the architect dealing with the problem of creating a new structure."[2] Herman Miller has a very broad based process to ensure that its vision and values are reexamined on an annual basis. It takes the form of a renewal survey that is filled out by all employee-owners. (All employees with more than a year of service become shareholders.) A recent survey included a letter from Dick Ruch, CEO, saying, "I have shared my commitment that Herman Miller be a learning organization. In order to learn, we need to listen to each other. The Renewal Survey is a tool for everyone to talk about what we are doing right and what we can do better."[3]

The Herman Miller survey was broken down into four sections, which were entitled:

[1]Reprinted with the permission of The Free Press, a Division of Macmillan, Inc. from *On Leadership* by John W. Gardner. Copyright © 1990 by John W. Gardner, pp. 13 and 192.

[2]Noel M. Tichy and Mary Anne Devanna, *The Transformational Leader*, John Wiley and Sons, New York, 1986, pp. 146 and 130. Copyright © 1986 by Noel M. Tichy and Mary Anne Devanna, with permission.

[3]Dick Ruch, "Renewal Survey 1990," Herman Miller Company Confidential Survey, p. 1.

- "About Me"
- "About My Work Team Leader"
- "About Senior Management"
- "About Herman Miller Values"

Herman Miller is on the leading edge in terms of participatory management. In return, it gets tremendous commitment from its people. And the trend appears to be going its way.

Rx for Leaders No. 1 Install a process that ensures a continuing renewal and revitalization of your vision and values. A questionnaire to all employees may seem superfluous, but the potential payoff in employee commitment makes it worth considering.

The Renewal Process at Phillips Petroleum

Normal turnover in management and the need to drive the vision through the entire organization provide strong reasons for the corporate renewal process to constantly extend participation and ownership in the vision and strategic plan. Phillips Petroleum, whose vision statement was examined in Chap. 3, provides a good model to use to examine the vision renewal process.

In February of 1990, Phillips CEO Pete Silas held a senior management conference to reexamine Phillips' corporate vision statement. The group consisted of Glenn Cox, his chief operating officer, and more than 30 top executives of the corporation. The group was slightly larger than the original group discussed in Chap. 3, and there had been some turnover in management. Overall, almost one-third of those present had not attended the first meeting.

Several introductory presentations provided the attendees with the required background information to bring everybody up to date on corporate performance and outlook. The presentations covered Phillips' longer-term financial performance and projections, a current economic and energy forecast, and a presentation on shareholder perspective. Pete Silas and Glenn Cox both made 15- to 20-minute presentations on their personal priorities for the corporation. This was followed by a summary of the confidential questionnaires that had been completed by each of the attendees prior to the meeting (see Chap. 12).

> **Rx for Leaders No. 2**   Remember, information is power. If you really want your people to help you on something as fundamental as reviewing your corporate vision, you have to give them the same breadth of information available to you. Everyone should be playing with the same deck.

Corporate Mission

The heart of the Phillips Petroleum Company renewal session included an in-depth review of each element of the Phillips' corporate vision statement, as well as a probing of corporate opportunities and obstacles. The special- focus subject of the session was "strategic intent" (discussed in Chap. 3). Teams were formed, and after short introductory presentations they broke out independently to consider the following questions:

- Does our current mission statement adequately address strategic intent?

- If so, how valid and complete is our current mission statement on a scale of 1 to 10? What needs to be added or changed to increase the rating to a 9 or 10?

- If not, what is our corporate strategic intent? How would you incorporate it into our current mission statement?

The clear consensus of the Phillips break-out teams was that the current mission statement did not contain an adequate expression of strategic intent. The groups felt not only that such a statement was needed but that it should be prominently positioned. The teams agreed that it should contain the concept of leadership or top performance. The final output from Pete Silas and the meld group, along with the original mission statement, is shown in Fig. 13-1.

The statement of *What We Are* identified Phillips' golden goose as integrated operations and was not touched. But the mission was sharpened. Silas' meld group liked the phrase "top performer in each of our businesses." But some felt that instead of *"the* top performer" it should read *"a* top performer" to be more in line with Phillips' size and relative capabilities. Another group felt that the word *"be"* should be changed to *"become,"* which would imply that it would take time to achieve its goal.

Silas listened to all sides of the argument and finally selected the wording as shown. He felt *"the* top performer" was the goal to which he

Original Mission

WHAT WE ARE...

An integrated petroleum company that explores for, produces, and upgrades oil and natural gas into petroleum products and chemicals for our customers.

OUR MISSION IS...

To enhance the value of our shareholders' investment by using the strengths of our people and our integrated operations to provide our customers with products that are high in quality and competitive in price.

Revised Mission

OUR MISSION IS...

To be the top performer in each of our businesses in order to enhance the value of our shareholders' investment.

We will utilize the teamwork of our people and the strengths of our integrated operations to provide our customers with products that are high in quality and competitive in price.

Figure 13-1. Phillips Petroleum Company original and revised mission statements.

wanted Phillips management to aspire, even if it was never achieved. He pointed out that "the top performer" did not have to be the biggest and could meet the challenge of top performance by a combination of being the most profitable, the best operator, the safest, the most environmentally concerned, and so forth. Further, he felt that the phrase "to become" was indefinite as to time. Silas contended that the real goal was "to *be* the top performer," even if it took a long time to get there and to *remain* the top performer. They certainly would not get there if the goal was not clear in everyone's mind. The management discussion was good, the points of view were ably presented, and the leader's decision was definitive.

The second change was championed by Glenn Cox, Phillips' president and chief operating officer. He and many others wanted to emphasize the importance of *teamwork*. Not only was the word itself inserted, but also the original mission was broken into two sentences to give it even greater emphasis.

> **Rx for Leaders No. 3**   Give your people a chance to provide input, not to vote.

Values and Beliefs

The next discussion focused on Phillips' values and beliefs. The questions for the break-out sessions were a little different:

- Are there any significant beliefs that have been omitted? Are there too many? Should any be revised or eliminated?
- On a scale of 1 to 10, how well are we living up to each of our corporate beliefs?
- Regarding each belief, what action is necessary to increase the rating to the 9 or 10 level?

The original and revised values and beliefs are shown in Fig. 13-2. There were no additions or deletions. In fact, it was strongly felt among the group that the values and beliefs of the company should have great stability, although slight revision or resequencing might be appropriate from time to time. Only two were modified:

- Original value number 6, "Supporting individual creativity and innovation," was strengthened by replacing the word "supporting" with "encouraging"; and the importance of team effort in a highly integrated, capital-intensive business was noted by deemphasizing "individual" and emphasizing "teamwork."
- In original value number 7, "providing our customers with top quality products and services" was changed to "total quality in everything we do." This is certainly broader and in line with the present worldwide emphasis on total quality management.

There were also some changes in the sequence of the values. "Maintaining a safe work environment" moved up from number 3 to number 1 and "Protecting the environment" moved up from number 8 to number 3. Also moved up significantly was "Communicating openly and honestly," from number 5 to number 2. The resequencing simply represented an opportunity to give special emphasis to certain values at a given point in time.

Original Values

WE BELIEVE IN...

- Treating one another with respect
- Giving equal opprtunity to every employee
- Maintaining a safe work environment
- Conducting ourselves ethically and responsibly
- Communicating openly and honestly
- Supporting individual creativity and innovation
- Providing our customers with top quality products and services
- Protecting the environment
- Contributing to the quality of life wherever we operate

Revised Values

WE BELIEVE IN...

- (3)* ■ Maintaining a safe work environment
- (5) ■ Communicating openly and honestly
- (8) ■ Protecting the environment
- (1) ■ Treating one another with respect
- (2) ■ Giving equal opportunity to every employee
- (4) ■ Conducting ourselves ethically and responsibly
- (6) ■ Encouraging creativity, innovation, and teamwork
- (7) ■ Providing our customers with total quality in everything we do
- (9) ■ Contributing to the quality of life wherever we operate

*Position in original values

Figure 13-2. Phillips Petroleum Company original and revised values.

Phillips gave evidence of its values at work in the marketplace in August 1990, when gasoline prices were skyrocketing in response to the Iraqi-induced oil crisis. *The Wall Street Journal* noted on August 10th, "Phillips Petroleum Company, which led the price cutting with a 4.5-cent cut Wednesday, said yesterday it was further reducing prices an average of 1.8 cents a gallon. A number of other major companies have said they were capping gasoline prices for some time."[4] It was a case of the dwarf leading the giants. Phillips not only saved its customers millions of dollars; it saved the customers of the other major firms an even larger sum. Phillips' actions were certainly in line with the values of "conducting ourselves ethically and responsibly" and "providing our customers with total quality in everything we do," which implies a fair price for value received.

Rx for Leaders No. 4   Test your values in the workplace. Do they affect the actions of your people? Phillips passed the test.

Long-Term Goals

Phillips asked itself about its long-term goals by posing the following questions to the break-out teams:

- Are there any significant goals that have been omitted? Have any been achieved or are no longer valid?

- On a scale of 1 to 10, how well are we meeting each of our corporate goals?

- Regarding each goal, what action is necessary to improve the rating to the 9 or 10 level?

The original and revised goals are shown in Fig. 13-3. The break-out teams did not feel that any significant goals had been omitted. But one had been partially achieved and so was no longer valid.

Utilizing a rationale developed by the break-out teams, Silas and the meld group decided that the goals should be less quantitative and specific. More quantitative targets could be addressed in supporting tactics and accountability statements. With regard to original goal number 2, Phillips had already reduced its debt below the $4 billion target. An improved and more permanent long-term goal was finally worked out and restated as "Maintain financial flexibility and consistently fund our capital program." The meld team felt that a set of strategies and specific tactics could be developed, monitored, and revised over time that would

---

[4]"White House Move Comes As Several Companies Reduce Gasoline Prices," *The Wall Street Journal,* August 10, 1990, p. A3, with permission.

Original Corporate Goals

(1) ■ Provide shareholder total return in the top 25 percent of the industry

(2) ■ Improve financial flexibility by reducing debt toward $4 billion and by increasing equity to $3 billion

(3) ■ Keep operations strong while maintaining high standards of safety, ethics, and environmental compliance

(4) ■ Use technology to improve competitive position

(5) ■ Build employee commitment and loyalty, while providing opportunity

(6) ■ Enhance customer relationships with quality goods and services

Revised Corporate Goals

(1)* ■ Provide shareholder total return in top 25 percent of the industry

(3) ■ Achieve and maintain the highest standards of safety, ethics, total quality and environmental performance in all operations

(4) ■ Improve competitive performance through a more effective utilization of technology

(5) ■ Build employee commitment and loyalty through opportunity and communications

(6) ■ Satisfy customer requirements through continuous quality improvement

(2) ■ Maintain financial flexibility and consistently fund our capital program

*Position in original goals

Figure 13-3. Phillips Petroleum Company original and revised corporate goals.

allow Phillips to achieve this more flexibly stated but very important corporate goal.

The group also decided that if the first two goals were perceived to be financial, Phillips could be misread both inside and outside the corporation as a financially driven operation. "Financial flexibility" was changed to the last goal. The first goal, which was unchanged, was characterized as a shareholder goal as opposed to a financial goal.

Original goal number 3 was revised to put the emphasis on "Achieve(ing) and maintain(ing) the highest standard of safety" rather than "Keep(ing) operations strong." The phrase "total quality" was added to emphasize this major new thrust. Finally, the group found the phrase "environmental compliance" to be too weak and replaced it with "highest standards of environmental performance in all operations." The goal was also elevated in importance from number 3 to number 2.

Between the development of the original plan and the February planning conference, a major disaster befell Phillips' Houston Chemical Complex. There were over twenty deaths, and the whole facility was destroyed. Safety moved even higher among the corporate values and goals, although it had been prominently represented in the original plan. Despite the disaster, Phillips appeared among *Fortune*'s "Most Admired Companies" in the petroleum industry for the first time. Their statement of strategic intent makes it clear that Phillips' management intends to move higher.

Rx for Leaders No. 5   Make your goals long term and directional. You can be specific and quantitative in your tactics and budget— in fact, the more so the better!

Opportunities and Obstacles

The session on opportunities and obstacles required the members of the break-out teams, all of whom represented individual business units or corporate staff groups, to assess opportunities across business unit lines. The questions in this session included the following:

- What are the five major business opportunities for Phillips in the 1990s? List in order of significance.

- What are the five major business obstacles for Phillips in the 1990s? List in order of significance.

- As a result of these opportunities and obstacles, which of our business lines have the most opportunity for profitable growth? Which have the least? Explain.

In effect, the teams were asked to look at the business portfolio as corporate general managers. They were to look across the panorama of business opportunities available to Phillips, assess the major internal or external obstacles, and decide how they would place their bets in terms of future profit growth. While the team answers are confidential, there was a clear consensus on where the opportunities and related profits could be found. The business unit managers had no problem breaking rank and endorsing the corporate perspective.

The various opinions offered and the consensus reached provided valuable input to Pete Silas and Glenn Cox that would not otherwise have been available. Phillips senior management was extremely pleased with the meeting, since it provided an opportunity to review and renew their corporate vision.

For a third of the attendees, this was their first meeting related to the corporate vision statement, and it provided them with insight into and a voice in the future of the corporation. Each attendee was asked to complete an "Assessment of Meeting Quality" questionnaire (see Fig. 13-4). On a scale of 1 to 20, the average evaluation was 18+. Question G asked, "How frequently should this kind of meeting be held?" All respondents felt that some type of renewal meeting should be held annually.

Rx for Leaders No. 6   Take the time to get a confidential evaluation and suggestions for improvement when you hold a key company meeting. Your people appreciate being asked, and your meetings will get better and better. Ask and you shall receive.

Assessment of Meeting Quality

Name _____ Date _____

Your candid comments regarding the effectiveness of this meeting are very important and will be treated confidentially.

A. Evaluation of the overall meeting (20 is highest)

20 19 18 17 16 15 14 13 12 11 10 9 8 7 6 5 4 3 2 1

B. What were the benefits of this meeting for you?

C. Was there any part of our discussion that was unproductive or could have been omitted?

D. What was *not* discussed that needs to be?

E. As a result of this conference, what is your understanding of our vision?

F. As a result of our discussion, what are the three most important action steps we need to take?

G. How frequently should this kind of meeting be held?

Please use the back for other comments.

Figure 13-4. Form for assessment of meeting quality.

The specific questions Phillips addressed were very helpful in reviewing its vision and values, but many other questions might serve that same purpose. Here are a few:

- What are the critical dynamics of our organization's environment? How do things really work? How do we make money?

- What trends are changing the nature of our industry? What represents the state-of-the-art in the industry? Does it pose opportunities or threats?

- What are our competitors doing? Are they gaining competitive advantage at our expense? Are we seeking new ways to gain our own advantage?

- What do our customers really want? How do they value what we offer? Can we add greater value?

- How is our organization distinctive and unique? What opportunities does our distinctiveness afford us?

- What are our most important and dominant capabilities, skills, and relationships? Can we further exploit them? Do we sufficiently understand them?

- If I could rewrite the history of my own achievements or of those of our industry, our organization, or our people, what would I change?[5]

Linking Vision and Compensation

Whenever a significant change is made in the corporate vision statement, the incentive compensation plan needs to be considered and probably changed. If incentive compensation does not link well with the strategic plan (which is the implementation vehicle for the corporate vision), it sends extremely confusing signals to the managers in the organization. The incentive plan (like the corporate organization structure) should be put into close harmony with the corporate vision and strategic plan at the time it is developed, and it should be kept in close harmony thereafter.

Rx for Leaders No. 7   Keep your incentive compensation plan closely linked to your vision and strategic plan. It just makes good cents!

---

[5]From *Creating Excellence* by Craig R. Hickman and Michael A. Silva. Copyright © 1984 by Craig R. Hickman and Michael A. Silva. Used by permission of New American Library, a division of Penguin Books USA Inc., pp. 165–166.

Linking Vision and Leadership at Outboard Marine Corporation, Rubbermaid, and Herman Miller

One goal of the vision development and renewal process is to demonstrate leadership at many levels. When Jim Chapman became CEO of Outboard Marine Corporation in January 1990, he told his people his goal was leadership—not just industry leadership, but general business leadership, which he expressed as a product and financial leadership achieved through total quality and empowered people. To emphasize this change, Chapman no longer has a planning process or planning meetings. He calls the process his leadership process and conducts it through regularly scheduled leadership meetings. He has tried to put the emphasis on the purpose of planning rather than on planning itself. This small but significant change appeals to many who tend to look down on planning but aspire to be leaders.

Chapman's personal corporate renewal process began in 1990, the year he became CEO. During that year, he visited every OMC plant and office in the world. He personally called on every investor of any size, institutional or other. He also endured a gut-wrenching year as industry sales dropped approximately 35 percent due to a slowing economy, rising interest rates, increased reluctance on the part of banks to make consumer loans, and finally the Iraq oil crisis. While OMC's market share increased, Chapman was forced to do some serious restructuring and record a large loss in his first year as CEO.

Difficulties did not alter his goal of general business leadership. Chapman set up visits with the CEOs of two distinctly different leading American corporations: Rubbermaid and Herman Miller. The two companies are in OMC's general size range, and both had been elected members of *Fortune*'s "Most Admired Companies." In letters to each of the CEOs, Chapman characterized the impetus of his visit as a desire "to learn the secrets of your success." Here is a sampling of what he discovered.

When he became CEO of Rubbermaid, Stanley Gault proceeded very quickly to make it one of only seven companies elected to *Fortune*'s "Most Admired Companies" five times or more. Gault emphasized product quality and market leadership. He saw the computer as the foundation of the customer partnership, in that it linked the customer directly with Rubbermaid and made the firm very easy to do business with. He also initiated and developed a competitive analysis system that was continually sharpened in a series of quarterly and annual reviews with each of his business unit managers.

Gault's new-product development goal was to draw 30 percent of all revenues from products announced in the last 5 years. The goal was reinforced through a series of monthly, quarterly, and annual reviews. Rubbermaid has no corporate strategic planning department, by design. All planning is done on the operating unit level, with the corporate officers responsible for review and general coordination. Gault holds approximately 75 meetings a year with security analysts and large shareholders to maintain a high stock price and enhance shareholder value. Employee communication programs are given the same emphasis through a number of different means. Chapman's overall impression was that the company was clearly market- and customer-driven and that Gault had tenaciously built structures in all parts of the company to ensure that it remained that way.

Herman Miller characterizes itself as "a research driven...manufacturer of furniture and furniture systems...unusual in its emphasis on its people...participative management, and employee stock ownership."[6] Chapman found that to be an excellent characterization.

Product designs are advanced and are often done at Herman Miller in conjunction with renowned external industrial designers. While highly regarded internationally for its product design, Herman Miller is equally well known for its emphasis on people and participative management. It has been recognized as one of the "hundred best companies to work for in America," it has been listed twice among *Fortune*'s "Most Admired Companies," and it received *Business Ethics* magazine's 1989 Excellence in Ethics Award for expanding the concept of employee ownership. Herman Miller has a highly participative management style backed up by the Scanlon Plan (a quarterly incentive bonus program in addition to each employee's base salary), a very extensive suggestion program, stock ownership for all employees, and "silver parachutes" for all its people. These silver parachutes represent an extension of the more common golden parachutes normally restricted to key executives in case of a takeover.

Financial performance was not even mentioned during Chapman's meeting, although Herman Miller's record is outstanding. Net sales of $50 million in 1976 grew to $250 million in 1981, and $793 million in 1989. The compound annual growth in sales between 1979 and 1989 was 16.3 percent. Net income grew a little faster, at 17.4 percent. But numbers did not run the company. It was driven by research and design balanced with an emphasis on people and participative management.

---

[6]"Herman Miller is Built on Its People, Research, and Designs," Herman Miller Company News Release, March 21, 1990, p. 1, with permission.

Rubbermaid is strongly market- and customer-driven. Herman Miller is research-, design-, and people-driven. But both have leaders who have a clear vision of where they are going and a set of values that give them and their people guidance along the way. In each case one of those values was a quality product; otherwise, their routes to excellence were quite different.

Instead of only two ways, I suspect there may be a hundred ways to achieve excellence as long as they are based on sound leadership, clear vision, a shared set of values, dedication to quality, and tenacity to goals.

Rx for Leaders No. 8   Pick a path to success that suits your company and be tenacious. There are a lot of paths toward excellence, but they all seem to include quality and a high regard for your people.

14

Sustaining the Corporate Vision and Values over Time

An IBM Case History

"If we look at the array of societies described by historians and anthropologists, we cannot find an instance of a healthy society in which humans have not devised a framework of values, norms of conduct, a moral order. When the community's broad consensus disintegrates or loses its force, the society sickens. People no longer find meaning in their lives. Nothing holds together. In describing such disintegration in Athens after the Peloponnesian Wars, Gilbert Murray introduced the great phrase 'the failure of nerve'."[1]

JOHN W. GARDNER

[1]Reprinted with the permission of The Free Press, a Division of Macmillan, Inc. from *On Leadership* by John W. Gardner, p. 76. Copyright © 1990 by John W. Gardner.

Chapter 2 described the origin of the IBM vision and values. This chapter revisits IBM and asks the question whether a great corporation, like a great society, can sustain its vision, values, and vitality over time, or if it must inevitably experience a failure of nerve. The case history should prove instructive for other firms, regardless of their size.

When Tom Watson, Jr. took over as IBM's CEO in 1956, sales had not yet reached $1 billion. By the time he retired in 1971, he had expanded the company eightfold, and sales had reached $7.5 billion. Watson's successors also did quite well and have increased IBM's sales almost tenfold since he retired. IBM was certainly on its way toward achieving Tom Watson, Sr.'s aspiration to "be the biggest business on earth."

IBM stock had the highest market value of any stock in the world for almost the entire period from 1967 (just after its landmark System 360 was announced) to 1987, the beginning of a severe decline for the entire U.S. computer industry. No other stock has been virtual king for 20 years, and probably none ever will be again. IBM could lay claim during that period to being the "most respected company in the world" in line with its unwritten vision statement (see Chap. 2).

But the lustre that surrounded the IBM name has been tarnished since the late 1980s. This chapter will first examine IBM's track record since the introduction of the computer in the early 1950s. We will also examine IBM's strategic position today.

Market value may be the ultimate corporate measurement when examining the total U.S. or world economy. In other measures of respect IBM won first-place rankings also. It was *Fortune*'s "Most Admired Company" from 1983 to 1986 and still ranked as one of the top 10 in 1987. In measures of size, IBM consistently had the largest net profit and also the largest operating cash flow of any company in the world (net profit plus depreciation exceeded $10 billion annually). It was these profits and cash flows that funded IBM's phenomenal growth in line with its long-standing corporate goal, "To sustain our profitability which funds our growth."

The Strategic Health of IBM's U.S. Competitors

To evaluate IBM's long-term performance record, it is necessary to examine the strategic health of its significant competitors. The driving force for IBM in this battle of titans was its number 1 goal, "To be the leader in products and services excelling in quality and innovation."

Among the Dead or Departed from the computer market battlefield are some proud warriors: GE, Honeywell, Raytheon, RCA, Philco, and Xerox (see Fig. 14-1). All but Philco made the list of the top 100 indus-

Strategic Health of IBM's Competitors	

Dead or Departed
 	
• GENERAL ELECTRIC
• HONEYWELL
• PHILCO
• RAYTHEON
• XEROX
	Retreating or Seriously Wounded
	
	• CONTROL DATA
	• UNISYS
	  - BURROUGHS
	  - SPERRY RAND
	• WANG

Prognosis Uncertain • NCR	**Newer to the Battle** • DIGITAL EQUIPMENT (DEC) • HEWLETT-PACKARD (H-P) • AMDAHL (1975) * • CRAY COMPUTER (1976) • APPLE COMPUTER (1977) • COMPAQ COMPUTER (1983)

* Year of initial sales for second generation competitors.

Figure 14-1.

trial companies in the United States (in terms of market value) at least once. Looking at the overall period from the end of World War II to the present time, GE stands out as one of the best-managed companies in the world. Yet its entry into battle with IBM resulted in a sound drubbing for GE and a tremendous reduction in the company's market value during that period.

A common characteristic of this group of companies is that they were unfocused in their approach to computers. Computers were considered just another business opportunity, as opposed to the only business. The computer business requires monogamy; extramarital affairs are not tolerated. IBM has always understood that.

The Retreating or Seriously Wounded include Control Data, the first new company to enter the computer battle after World War II. Its stock has been declining since 1987, it lost money from 1985 to 1989, and it is now almost out of the computer business. Unisys, the result of a merger of Burroughs and Sperry-Rand, has presented a test of whether a high-profile general businessman–public servant (who knows nothing about computers) can lead a major computer company successfully. The answer appears to be no. The problems certainly did not start with former CEO, Mike Blumenthal, but he was not able to solve them. Unisys' future appears bleak.

Wang lost money in 3 of the last 4 years. In 1992, it filed for bankruptcy protection. Its founder, Dr. An Wang, has departed. Like Blumenthal, R. W. Miller, Wang's new CEO, did not grow up with computers the way most of his competitors did. The losses of Control Data, Unisys, and Wang since 1985 provide one measure of how difficult the U.S. computer market has become.

NCR is in the Prognosis-Uncertain category despite its acquisition by AT&T. It has been in the business machine–computer industry longer than any other company, and it has been a survivor. In spite of that, its computer sales today are about the same as those of Compaq, which made its first sale in 1982. NCR will never be a major player in the industry.

Rx for Leaders No. 1   Keep in mind that the computer business is not the only one that requires monogamy. Extramarital affairs are not easily tolerated in any business.

All IBM's newer competitors prospered until 1987, which marked the beginning of a severe test for the whole industry. Hewlett-Packard and especially DEC have seen their market value deteriorate since 1987. This is representative of their perceived market position and expected performance.

Several additional companies appeared on the computer market battlefield between 1975 and 1980. Amdahl and Compaq might be considered technology copiers to some degree in that their machines emulate or are compatible with IBM's. Apple and Cray, on the other hand, must be considered technological innovators. They all have had enviable performance records. Yet all those entering the market before 1980 hit the wall in 1987, just as IBM and DEC did (although Hewlett-Packard has fared better). The only one to escape the 1987 downturn was Compaq, which entered the market in 1983 in the high-growth microcomputer end of the business. Compaq had enviable growth and profitability until 1991, when it also hit the wall.

All six companies Newer to the Battle share one attribute that is decidedly different from IBM's early competitors. The new competitors are all highly focused. With the exception of Hewlett-Packard, they make computing their only business.

In this massive 30 to 40 year competitive struggle, IBM's compelling goal "to be the leader in products and services" was always foremost in the minds of its leaders and its people. If IBM loses its long-term leadership, it will be because of a failure in execution, not aspiration. Now, a look to the future.

Market Position and Power

The computer battlefield has been littered with the dead and wounded. A review of the survivors is appropriate. A critical indicator of overall performance is relative market *power* or position, traditionally evaluated in terms of market share. The computer industry is generally divided into three major segments: microcomputers, minicomputers, and mainframes. IBM was number 1 in each major segment in 1990, the beginning of the decade. But it wasn't always so. In each market somebody else had beaten IBM in terms of market entry and early market dominance. Sperry-Rand was an early leader in mainframes, Digital Equipment in minicomputers, and Apple in microcomputers.

Some key quantitative indicators of future market position in any industry are: (1) current market position or share (perhaps best measured by total revenues in a multi-market environment), (2) cost structure or profitability, and (3) current investment in the future (partially measured by total research, development, and engineering expenditures).

The main thrust of Fig. 14-2 is to examine the long-term global outlook for the major players in the U.S. computer industry. The competitors are listed in terms of total revenue for the same year, 1990. While

Company	Revenues (billions)	Net Profit Margin	R&D
IBM	$69.0	8.7%	9.5%
HP	13.2	5.6	10.3
DEC	12.9	4.1	12.5
Unisys	10.1	—	7.4
NCR	6.3	5.9	8.0
Apple	5.6	8.5	8.6
Compaq	3.6	12.0	5.2

Figure 14-2. Indicators of future market position. [*All data from* Value Line (*1990 actual*).]

IBM never achieved world leadership in revenue among all corporations, it is 5 times the size of its nearest competitors in the computer industry, Hewlett-Packard (HP) and Digital Equipment (DEC). As the 1980s drew to a close, only Compaq had higher net profit margins than IBM, with Apple not far behind. In R&D expenditures as a percentage of sales, only DEC led IBM, with HP just behind. In total dollars, IBM's R&D expenditures were roughly 5 times those of any of its competitors—in line with their difference in sales. This was the domestic competitive outlook as IBM entered the nineties. But a look at the larger picture is necessary.

The Global Picture

IBM vision has always been global. The word "International" in its name has been a mandate. Over 60 percent of IBM's revenues come from overseas, where its margins have historically been higher than those at home. Worldwide computer industry sales in 1990 were estimated at about $150 billion, with almost two-thirds from outside the United States. Europe accounts for about half the outside sales, and Japan and the rest of the world for the other half.

In Europe, IBM is approximately 4 times the size of its nearest competitor, Siemens, closely followed by DEC. An indication of IBM's strength in the European market is that it is the second largest exporter in Germany, and Germany is the largest exporter in Europe.

Growth in the European computer market has stopped abruptly, however, with Bull, Olivetti, and the computer division of NV Phillips losing money and beginning the significant restructuring that has recently characterized U.S. companies. As in the United States, mergers can be expected, and another three to five competitors should disappear.

As the Iron Curtain fell, IBM moved aggressively into the former U.S.S.R. and Eastern Europe. Tom Watson, Jr., had been ambassador to the Soviet Union after he left IBM, so the company had some prior connections to the East. In 1991, IBM established the first wholly owned U.S. subsidiary in the Soviet Union. In Czechoslovakia, IBM has established another subsidiary with over 60 people. A Hungarian subsidiary is developing a dealer network, and in Germany IBM is setting up a joint venture with Robotron, the area's largest computer manufacturer. Yet another sign of globalization is IBM's transfer in 1990 of its communications business to Europe, marking the first time it has moved a product group outside the United States. The group generates about $5 billion of revenue a year.

The Japanese

IBM is not about to lay its global vision aside easily. But the Japanese pose a distinct threat, both real and long-term. Unlike IBM's European competitors, all the Japanese companies were profitable until 1992. Facing extreme pressures on the pricing of its microprocessors, Fujitsu announced the closing of its San Diego semiconductor plant and has seen demand for its mainframes slip.

The Japanese computer industry has begun to suffer the demand and price slippage that struck the United States in 1987. Still, Fujitsu has revenues equal to about 30 percent of IBM's total revenues and is IBM's largest global competitor. Fujitsu's takeover of ICI made it number 2 in the world, ahead of DEC and HP. More recently, Fujitsu bought Nokia Data, Scandinavia's largest computer manufacturer. The day before IBM announced its new large mainframe line, Fujitsu announced its own line. Hitachi, NEC, and Amdahl (40 percent owned by Fujitsu) are also formidable rivals.

The Japanese market had been growing at twice the rate of the U.S. market (with Europe and the rest of the world in between), allowing the Japanese competitors to generate higher profits, while U.S. manufacturers face strong profit pressure. At the small end of the product line, NEC and Toshiba are prominent in the PC market. Toshiba is the clear leader in portable computers. A key IBM goal of the nineties will be to duplicate its PC performance of the eighties, coming from nowhere to market leadership in laptops and notebook computers. To try to catch up, IBM will base its laptop and smaller computer development labs in Japan, where it hopes to be infused with Japan's culture of consumer electronics. This represented another step in IBM's global commitment.

The battle between IBM and the Japanese will be on the frontiers, the top, and the bottom of the computer spectrum, as well as on the extension of the computer into new application areas. Image processing represents another frontier. It is based on processing images such as fingerprints, X-rays, and charge card slips rather than letters or numbers. Image processing has been called a "resource hog," requiring complex systems and hardware and facilitation by massively parallel processing. Some see this area as a potential for returning the computer industry to its high-growth days.

The ultimate competition with the Japanese may be for the best minds. "To the dismay and chagrin of many scientists, leading Japanese computer and electronics companies are opening laboratories to do basic research in the United States, luring some of the most creative American computer scientists to work for them. Some researchers and economists see this as a direct threat."[2] NEC recently opened a lab in Princeton, New Jersey, Matsushita will open one near San Francisco, and Canon will open one in Stanford, California. Mitsubishi, Fujitsu, and Ricoh are deliberating setting up their own outposts in the United States. IBM has set up new labs in both Japan and England and has others spread around the globe. The battle will be global, long, and difficult.

R&D Investments

IBM's expenditures for research, development, and engineering totaled about $7 billion annually in the late eighties. Its R&D expenditures were almost twice the combined expenditures of its traditional competitors in total market value, Exxon and GE. The task of managing this R&D investment is difficult to comprehend. The expenditures are about the same as the annual sales of such outstanding companies as Merck, Ralston-Purina, and Emerson Electric (all Fortune 100 companies).

IBM's continuing high level of R&D investments has long been seen as a critical support to its number 1 goal: "to be the leader in products and services excelling in quality and innovation." The high priority of IBM's R&D program is also based on one of its three basic values, excellence—the conviction that an organization should pursue all tasks with the object of accomplishing them in a superior way.

There are those who believe that IBM does not get its money's worth from its R&D program. "IBM is constantly criticized for being behind in technology. It's a bum rap. Their sales and service stars have shone so bright that people often miss the company's luster in basic science. Further, IBM is not especially concerned with being first to market with a new technology, preferring, it seems, to let others test the market for them....Apple Computer founder Steve Jobs has said, 'IBM is a national treasure.'"[3]

IBM is clearly recognized by the scientific community as the number 1 or number 2 industrial contributor to basic research in the United States. IBM is also a recognized leader in advanced memory chip technology. While most of its competitors buy technology, IBM has maintained an active role in technologies it considers critical. A recent illustration of IBM's determination was a billion-dollar investment in an experimental x-ray technology to keep IBM and the United States from dependence on Japanese computer chips.

---

[2]Gina Kolata, "Japanese Labs in U.S. Luring America's Computer Experts," *The New York Times,* November 11, 1990, p. 1.

[3]From *The Renewal Factor* by Robert H. Waterman, Jr., p. 226. Copyright © 1987 by Robert H. Waterman, Jr. Used by permissin of Bantam Books, a division of Bantam Doubleday Dell Publishing Group, Inc.

> **Rx for Leaders No. 2**   Vote your R&D dollars in line with your corporate vision. Listen to the smart people like Steve Jobs.

Other Investments and Partnerships

IBM has balanced its R&D expenditures with another type of investment. Many years ago, IBM entered into an arrangement with Sears to market Prodigy, now the largest supplier to PC users of banking, shopping, games, and other services by telephone. Later IBM established an accord with AT&T in the area of network management. In July of 1991 it announced a broad technology agreement with Apple for the development of both hardware and software. The next day, IBM announced a joint production agreement with Siemens, the largest European computer manufacturer, to produce the world's most advanced computer memory chips. A $700 million plant will be constructed near Paris, which will cement IBM's presence in Europe even more strongly.

IBM is also making huge investments in software services and partnerships. Some analysts expect that 50 percent of computer industry investments will be in software and related services by 1993 (up from about 33 percent in 1981). IBM has publicly stated that it intends to shift the balance of its investments to software, up from 41 percent of total investments in 1989. Software will be yet another battleground of the nineties for IBM.

There have also been numerous IBM investment partnerships with smaller companies, including Supercomputer Systems, Inc., InterAct Corporation, PCO Inc., Polygen Corp., Interactive Images, and Transarc Corporation—to name just a few. Most of these relationships take the form of direct equity investments. Through 1989, IBM had established more than 75 equity investments worldwide, and the number has increased practically every month since then. Driving IBM's partnering efforts is its new number 1 goal announced by Akers in 1985: "to enhance customer relationships" by finding the best solution available to their customer's problems inside or outside of IBM. Combined with the former number 1 goal of product leadership and the shared value of excellence, these goals make up a powerful driving force in IBM.

> **Rx for Leaders No. 3**   Get moving, if you are not already started, toward building extensive global partnerships. IBM was global before the word was popularized and now has over 100 partnerships around the world.

IBM Image Shattered

IBM's global competitive environment as it entered the 1990s was certainly challenging but equally promising. It faced a set of domestic competitors each strong in their primary niche markets. It also faced a set of Japanese competitors gaining strength rapidly on the perimeter of the world market, the very large and the very small computers. But IBM was 5 times the size of its largest competitors. Its sales and research capabilities were strong and well funded. And it had built numerous worldwide partnerships with large and small companies to shore up areas of weakness. The critical weakness was that IBM's strategy had been built on a worldwide computer market that they expected to grow 10 to 15 percent a year. In fact, IBM had already hired the people and built the plants to accomodate that growth. But it didn't come.

Before the end of the first quarter of 1991, IBM indicated its earnings would plunge 50 percent for the quarter. It said the problem was that customers simply stopped buying, primarily because of the Middle East war and recession or recessionary fears worldwide. Only software, service, and the newly announced workstations escaped. The problem was worldwide, not just the United States. IBM almost immediately announced a job reduction program estimated at 20,000 people around the world. In late 1991 IBM announced a $3 billion charge to cover the job cuts, a major reorganization of its business, and a shattering loss for the year.

Market conditions did not improve in 1992. Provision was made for an additional 25,000 people to take early retirement in 1993, resulting in over 125,000 reduction since IBM's peak employment in 1985. Total worldwide employment would ultimately be about 275,000—down from a high of over 400,000. IBM also announced additional capacity reductions in worldwide manufacturing space, a total shrinkage of over 40 percent since 1985. Pretax charges taken in 1992 for these expected 1993 reductions totaled $11.4 billion. IBM finally announced a loss of $5 billion, the largest corporate loss ever reported at that time. IBM saw no sign of improvement in early 1993.

IBM stock fell over 20 percent in the two days after the December 1992 announcement to below $50 per share, partly because of the fear of a reduced dividend which was announced later. From its peak in 1987, the year the computer industry went into "intensive care," the stock had fallen from $175 a share, over 70 percent. In terms of market value, IBM had slipped from number 1 in the world over the preceding 20 years clear out of the top ten, a humbling fall for the blue giant. $1,000 invested in IBM in 1982 would be worth about $800 today, versus $13,000 if invested in Coca-Cola at that same time. IBM stock had fallen over 40 percent in 1992 alone. IBM competitors in mainframes and minicomputers fared even worse: DEC was off about 50 percent, Cray about 55 percent, and Amdahl about 65 percent. But Apple, Compaq, and Hewlett-Packard—all in personal computers and workstations (where the market remained stronger)—did far better than IBM.

This precipitous drop in profits presented a tremendous conflict to IBM. It brought two of its five goals into a confrontation with an equally important shared value, "Respect for the individual: Respect for the dignity and the rights of each person in the organization." The IBM goals involved were "to be the most efficient in everything we do" (productivity) and "to sustain our profitability which funds our growth."

The only way to restore IBM's traditional profitability and productivity was to reduce employment dramatically. The solution was to offer early retirement with very attractive financial incentives. Nobody was fired or forced to resign, but the pressure was certainly felt by some employees. Overall, however, IBM and most observers felt that respect for the individual was maintained even though the financial burden was very high, as reflected in restructuring charges. In light of the reversal of IBM's profitability and its staff reductions, a review of management and compensation seems called for.

Management

IBM's restructuring announcement indicated some significant changes in management direction and raised considerable speculation about management itself. Akers said IBM would be making a big shift from its previous mainframe computer core toward the software and services market. In line with this shift, IBM said it would cut spending on product development by about $1 billion in 1993, approximately 17 percent.

The December 1992 restructuring was only the latest step in IBM's 5-year downward spiral. Some large institutional shareholders were upset and vocal. Some felt that if Akers could not show signs of solving the puzzle soon, maybe it was time for a new CEO and reexamination of IBM's values or strategy. Others felt that Akers was slow in making bold market moves or the timely divestment of underperforming businesses and assets. This could be related to the IBM "fear of failure" (mentioned by Tom Watson, Jr., in Chap. 2) which can be a significant factor warring against bold initiatives.

No inside candidate is seen as having the required management experience and objectivity to address issues of this magnitude. While that kind of experience is also difficult to find outside, speculation centered around John Scully from Apple, Jack Welch from GE, or Welch's former CFO, Larry Bossidy, now CEO at Allied Signal. It would be a short list, in any case.

Despite its historical leadership in market value, profitability, and market share, IBM is not one of the leaders in management compensation. As *Business Week* has noted, "Lotus Development Corporation paid James P. Manzi roughly as much money in a single year, $26.3 million, as IBM's Thomas J. Watson, Jr., made in his 15 years at the helm of Big Blue—even allowing for inflation."[4] IBM apparently does not believe that CEOs should be paid like rock stars. John Akers averaged $1.7 million in cash compensation in 1989 and 1990. This compares to Tom Watson, Jr.'s average pay of $1.8 million (adjusted for inflation) in the time that he served as CEO. Compensation for upper management is good but conservative by most standards.

The payoff has not been in stock, either. None of IBM's CEOs has had a significant position in IBM stock since Tom Watson, Sr. Watson, Jr., has said that his father never owned more than 5 percent of the company, and none of the other CEOs has even approached that level. Akers presently owns about 44,000 shares in the company, and John Opel, the prior CEO, about 21,000 shares. At IBM, being CEO has been mainly about leadership, not money.

Rx for Leaders No. 4   Pay your people a little better and yourself a little bit less and you'll probably build a better team.

Competitive War

IBM's profit decline in 1991 and 1992 is undoubtedly its most significant setback in an otherwise outstanding 60-year history. And the battle is far from over.

In the remainder of the nineties, IBM will be fighting a competitive war of unprecedented magnitude. Competitive *wars* are fought for 10 to 20 years and consist of many battles that can consume the total resources of the competitors. These wars are fought to the company's death or surrender of one of the combatants. Most armies that have fought on two fronts have lost the war. IBM will be forced to fight on three fronts: the United States, Europe, and Japan. It will also fight in the traditional market segments: microcomputers, minicomputers, and mainframes. And there will be the war of the frontiers: laptops and notebooks, new forms of input such as image processing, as well as massively parallel computers (multiple computers linked in a parallel rather than sequential mode to solve problems more rapidly).

The question is whether any company can win a war with battles fought on so many different fronts over such a long period of time.

---

[4]"Putting a Price on CEOs," *Business Week*, October 21, 1988, pp. 34–36.

While the Japanese may well be the strongest long-term competitor, there will continue to be strong U.S. competitors in each segment of the market.

IBM hasn't lost one of these 10- to 20-year competitive wars yet, although it will certainly lose additional skirmishes and battles. Dan Mandresh, who follows IBM for Merrill Lynch, perhaps summed it up best. "There are problems endemic to the industry right now....[IBM] is still a $66 billion company and all that stands in the way of Japan's domination of our market."[5] If IBM loses the war, we lose the war as a nation.

A New Structure for New Threats

When IBM announced its restructuring in late 1991, it also announced a major reorganization to address the competitive war of the 1990s. Akers maintains that IBM lost contact with its customer somewhere in the 1970s and 1980s. When he took over in 1985, Akers made "enhancing customer relationship" goal number 1 above the four long-standing IBM goals reviewed in Chap. 2. Akers' recent restructuring of IBM permanently embedded the customer goal deep in the IBM organization structure. Over the years since the introduction of the computer in the 1950s, IBM has entered market after market in computer applications—from banking to grocery store checkouts to satellite tracking and control. It is now doing business in over 100 countries, and the break-up of the former U.S.S.R. and Eastern Europe will probably add another 25. Keeping track of who the customers are and what they need and then enhancing those relationships in a tightly centralized corporate structure had become almost impossible by the time Akers took the helm. Corporate gridlock was a real threat—some feel it occurred!

Akers' response to that threat was an almost complete reorganization of IBM into nine market- and product-oriented business units, each with its own financial reporting system and board of directors, to be managed to maximize individual return on assets. There will also be five geographic business units that will buy from the product units for subsequent sale and service in the marketplace. The reorganization certainly will allow IBM to improve its customer focus and bring decision making much closer to the marketplace. IBM headquarters will act more as a holding company, evaluating the current and anticipated performance of each business unit. The restructuring announcement in December of 1992 said IBM would take additional steps to further increase the autonomy of its business units.

---

[5]"Old Blue Gets Hit Again...," *The New York Times*, June 23, 1991, p. B2.

Aker's Resignation

In January of 1993, in the midst of IBM's record losses, restructuring, and reorganizing, the ax fell. Akers resigned or was forced to resign. Along with him went IBM's president, Jack Kuehler, and the CFO. Combined with the earlier departure of three senior vice presidents, IBM's top leadership was gone in a single year. IBM would not be the same company again.

What happened? Was it failure in vision or execution? It certainly was not a given competitor or group of competitors that could lay claim to IBM's defeat. The defeat came from within. Was it complexity? Did the task at hand simply become mind-boggling:

- Trying to be the world leader in all aspects of computer technology, moving at an explosive pace
- Reinvesting wisely their $10 billion cash flow each year
- Playing a leading national role in basic research
- Managing a $7 billion annual research and development budget
- Participating in and wanting to dominate all new computer applications from image processing to multimedia
- Doing business in practically every country in the world
- Entering into a hundred corporate partnerships all over the world, from Apple to PCO, Inc. to Siemens

Combining this complexity with IBM's highly centralized operating and decision-making style could well induce gridlock. Add a little"fear of failure," mentioned earlier in this chapter by Tom Watson, Jr., and gridlock becomes an even greater possibility.

Akers did not invent the complexity of the world he faced or the management structure he inherited, but he also did not solve them. His failure was first signaled by large shareholders and the press. In fact, by the time of Aker's resignation, there was a small cottage industry of IBM watchers, commentators, or vultures, depending on your viewpoint. Finally came Aker's resignation and the broad search for his successor.

Akers has some consolation, considering the fate of fellow CEOs in the computer industry. Departures have taken place in practically every company: founders Steve Jobs at Apple, An Wang at Wang, Kenneth Olsen at Digital Equiptment, plus Mike Blumenthal at Unisys, Rod Canion at Compaq, John Rollwagen at Cray, and Charles Exley, Jr., at NCR (acquired by AT&T). The only one to escape was John Young at Hewlett-Packard. He has a reputation of being a fine executive, and even here, the founders came back to sit with him during a couple of tough years. The industry has not been easy on its leaders.

Did IBM display a failure of nerve as described by Gilbert Murray earlier in this chapter? I believe so. Its response time to major changes in its industry environment was simply too slow. No matter what happens in the future, the IBM vision will be altered but probably not discarded. If IBM remains a single but highly decentralized company, the new leaders will most likely build on the existing vision but demonstrate clearly how the new vision differs. If one or more companies are spun off, there is an even greater chance of vision differentiation but still with a probable claim on their "blue-blooded" lineage.

So an era has ended. IBM as we have known it is dead. It has displayed "failure of nerve." But it will have successors, few or many. And life and growth will begin again. We should be so lucky as a nation to a dozen or even a halfdozen, IBMs with their world vision and outstanding performance.

Rx for Leaders No. 5 Look at IBM's victories and defeats from your own perspective. You have seen the same ups and downs in your company and industry. Note that when IBM's growth failed, everything came into question, including the survival of the CEO and the company. Growth is the key to corporate survival. Make your vision and values the keys to growth.

PART 4

Linking Vision to Traditional Strategic Planning and Other Types of Organizations

- Links the vision and values concept to more traditional aspects of strategic planning.
- Examines organizations other than large corporations.

15
Strategic Planning

Making the Vision a Reality

Jonathan Swift said that "vision is the art of seeing things invisible." Strategic planning is the management process aimed at making that vision a reality. The relationship of traditional strategic planning to the leader's vision is the subject of this chapter. Strategies and tactics, which are the core of the strategic plan, have been discussed earlier in Chap. 4. The use of strategies and tactics as the focus of stewardship was discussed in Chap. 12.

Planning is the Leader's Most Fundamental Function

The fundamental functions of management are generally held to be: *planning, organizing, directing (or motivating), and controlling.* Some people question whether direction or motivation is a fundamental function and which of the two functions is more appropriate. But there is little debate about planning, organizing, and controlling.

Planning is almost universally considered to be the leader's first and most critical management task. Likewise, the development of the leader's vision and values are the first and most important step in planning. It is in the vision and values that the leader lays out the most critical elements of the selected course for the future.

A corporation should not plan around the current organization. Instead, it should organize around the corporate strategy or plan.

Planning precedes organizing. Similarly, controlling is a key step in monitoring implementation for plan modification. Thus planning is first—not just in time but in logic and importance as well.

The leader's values are an appeal to the heart, and the leader's mission is an appeal to the intellect. Both values and mission are directed toward commitment. Corporate commitment represents acceptance of the leader's vision (values, mission, and goals)—the core of the leadership contract.

Rx for Leaders No. 1   Make sure planning takes the proper priority in your agenda. Planning is the leader's first and most fundamental task.

Formal and Informal Planning

Planning is the most fundamental function of leadership, but it is not always formal. While the unwritten, informal method of planning has a certain appeal in terms of flexibility and lack of bureaucracy, it has some overpowering weaknesses in terms of ambiguity, lack of consensus and commitment, and a consequent loss of management energy. Planning is the leader's primary function. The leader cannot avoid or escape the long-range implications of his or her decisions and actions. In this sense the leader always plans, one way or another, either formally or informally.

Furthermore, planning need not be formalized to as great a degree in a corporation that competes essentially in one product line, as opposed to a number of product lines in a number of markets. Apple, for instance, has always competed solely in the personal computer market. The level of planning required of Apple is modest relative to that of IBM, which competes in almost every market segment and in almost every application area. Size and geographic focus are other factors, with IBM's sales at over $60 billion and Apple's at less than one tenth of that. IBM is also in the components industry, whereas Apple is generally only producing an end product. Apple's recent effort to move its products more deeply into the business market will certainly require a higher level of planning. "Starting with the 1991 corporate business plan, more stringent controls are in place. And planning has become more of a discipline and less of a fantasy."[1]

---

[1]Barbara Buell, Jonathan B. Levine, and Neil Gross, "Apple: New Team, New Strategy," *Business Week*, October, 15, 1990, p. 92.

Even less formal planning is required by a company such as Compaq, whose cost-based strategy for a long time has been IBM compatibility at a lower price. Compaq's R&D expenditures as a percentage of sales are about 40 percent of IBM's expenditures. Its strategy was one not of innovation but rather of making a quick copy. And it has been extremely successful. With Compaq's attempts to innovate and expand into other markets, the level and degree of formality in planning will expand proportionately.

Rx for Leaders No. 2   Beware of the unwritten, informal method of planning and its weaknesses in terms of ambiguity. The plan should be written, but keep it short and simple.

The Purpose of Strategic Planning

The purposes of strategic planning, as seen from a historical perspective, were very basic:

- Improving operating decisions
- Delegating authority and responsibility
- Communicating

Improving Operating Decisions.   This emphasizes several points. Planning is not seen as a futuristic, academic exercise. It is not about the future—it is about today, and more importantly, about today's decisions. Drucker's perspective is that planning is not about future decisions, but about the futurity of today's decisions.

Delegating Authority and Responsibility.   The operating unit's strategic and operating authority come from the annual review and approval of plans. The strategic plan review process allows this very important delegation to the operating head without any abdication of corporate review and approval.

Communicating.   Communicating is an important purpose of planning in all organizations. When a corporation has three to four hundred thousand employees in over 100 countries, it becomes even more critical. Communication not only moves upward to top management, but also across to sister divisions or operations, to the managers and people within the organization and, finally, as appropriate, to customers and vendors.

A more current perspective of strategic planning includes the following:

- Allocating resources
- Creating clear strategic focus
- Forging management commitment

Allocating Resources.   This applies to both human and financial resources. While the allocation of resource is a fundamental purpose of planning, it is often overdone, particularly with regard to financial resources. If the underlying business or market concept of a plan is sound, financial resources should not be a problem even if marshaling them requires external funding, joint venturing, partnering, or some other form of acquiring additional capital. The use of the planning process as a means of rationing or refusing funding is negative and demoralizing. Business opportunities should be refused only because they lack fundamental soundness, not because there is inadequate funding available. This should be as true for the intrapreneur as the entrepreneur.

Creating Clear Strategic Focus.   The achievement of management consensus through a shared understanding of the external environment and relative competitive position is a fundamental purpose of effective planning. Achieving this consensus or focus may mean the actual loss of some members of the management team who cannot accept the selected direction. But that, too, can be a benefit. In effect, corporate planning becomes a shared learning process for corporate management.

Forging Management Commitment.   The objective of clear strategic focus is an equally clear management commitment or the will to make the corporation's mission and long-term goals a reality. The importance of this will to bring about a shared vision cannot be overstated. All the other purposes of planning support and are subservient to this final purpose.

From the point of view of the operator—whether at the corporate, group, or business unit level—there are many reasons to plan: to increase sales, to gain market share, to reduce costs, to increase profitability, to improve cash flow, to improve return on investment, and to reduce head count. Each of these represents very specific operating needs supportive of the overall health of the enterprise.

But the leader or CEO must take a longer view. This view includes the clarification of objectives, corporate renewal and continuity, improved long-term performance, management commitment, better resource allocation, diversification, and enhanced shareholder value. These goals address the long-term strategic health of the corporation.

Rx for Leaders No. 3   Take the longer view of strategic planning, including clarification of objectives, corporate renewal and continuity, and enhanced shareholder value. Make certain your planning process addresses these issues.

Leadership Tasks in Strategic Planning

The leader must address the following general tasks in any well-developed strategic planning process:

- Creating and renewing the overall corporate vision, including the corporate values, mission, and long-term goals
- Ensuring the development of the supporting business and financial implementation plans at the corporate and operating unit levels
- Effective and timely resolution of major corporate business issues, both opportunities and threats, consistent with the underlying corporate vision and business plan

In his book on management tasks, Drucker devotes a chapter to "Strategic Planning: The Entrepreneurial Skill."[2] In that chapter he emphasizes that strategic planning should not be confused with "a bundle of techniques," whether they involve the seven Ss, generic strategies, total quality management, matrices, cash cows, product life cycles, or specific tools for competitive analysis. He also points out that strategic planning is not forecasting. "Strategic planning is necessary precisely because we cannot forecast....Strategic planning does not deal with future decisions. It deals with the futurity of present decisions. [Finally] strategic planning is not an attempt to eliminate risk."[3] It is an attempt to address and manage risk better than one's competitors.

---

[2]Peter F. Drucker, *Management Tasks, Responsibilities, Practices,* Harper & Row, New York, 1974, p. v., with permission.

[3]Ibid, pp. 124–125.

Bennis and Nanus address the issue of what planning is rather than what it is not:

> In its most general sense, planning is nothing more than a process of making informed judgments about the future and acting on them. However, it can be institutionalized in a formal planning mechanism through which the organization identifies and evaluates new issues, designs and considers alternative policies, generates a consensus about appropriate actions, and provides legitimacy for major changes in direction. In a recent study by James Brian Quinn of nine large corporations, the most important contributions of formal planning processes were found to be the following:
>
> - They created a network of information that would not otherwise have been available.
> - They periodically forced operating managers to extend their horizons.
> - They required vigorous communications.
> - They systematically taught managers about the future.[4]

Rx for Leaders No. 4   Make planning a tool to help you manage risk and uncertainty better than your competitors. Use planning to extend your people's horizons and improve their communication with all of those vital to their strategic success.

The CEO's Increasing Involvement in Planning

The involvement of the leader in strategic planning is increasing. In a recent article in *The Wall Street Journal* based on a poll of CEOs, two major trends were noted in the last 5 years: more involvement with strategic planning and a greater concern about global competition. More than 20 percent of the responding CEOs saw even greater involvement with strategic planning in the next 5 years.[5]

Establishing the objectives, plans, and policies of the corporation is clearly more fundamental than directing the business or overseeing day-to-day operations, two of the CEO's other primary responsibilities.

---

[4]Excerpts from *Leaders: The Strategies for Taking Charge* by Warren Bennis and Burt Nanus, pp. 212–213. Copyright © 1985 by Warren Bennis and Burt Nanus. Reprinted by permission of HarperCollins Publishers Inc.

[5]Michael J. McCarthy, "A CEO's Life: Money, Security and Meetings," *The Wall Street Journal,* July 7, 1987, p. 31., with permission.

Furthermore, responsibility for long-range objectives and plans cannot be delegated. The CEO can and often does delegate day-to-day operations to the chief operating officer and responsibility for the financial planning and controls of the corporation to a chief financial officer. In fact, the CEO often delegates practically every other function in a very large corporation—with one exception. The CEO cannot delegate the responsibility for charting or planning the corporation's future. And even though responsibility for the planning *process* is delegated to a chief planning officer, the CEO can never delegate the *substance* of those plans and particularly the responsibility of being author and guardian of the corporation's vision and values.

Another vital responsibility of the CEO is communicating the corporation's strategic vision and values to relevant publics and constituencies to gain and maintain their continuing commitment. The corporate strategic vision, developed and carefully shaped by the CEO and the key leaders of the organization, is stillborn without attention to communication and commitment. Regardless of size and whether the organization is public or private, for-profit or not-for-profit, gaining acceptance of the strategic vision of the enterprise is a major responsibility of the CEO.

The leader is *selling*—as is everyone else in the corporation, to the extent that they want to be a leader. To be effective, the corporate vision must be communicated to a number of critical audiences: to the board of directors for review and counsel, to all executive and management personnel to guide their implementation efforts, to employees for understanding and commitment, and to stockholders and the financial community to advise them of the company's broad direction.

Rx for Leaders No. 5 Delegate everything else if you have to but don't delegate the responsibility for charting or planning the corporation's future. Gaining acceptance of the shared values of the enterprise is the major responsibility of the CEO.

Planning Is What the CEO Says It Is

In the final analysis, planning is what the CEO says it is in any given corporation. There are many different aspects of planning—strategic, business, operational, resource, facility, human resource, financial, and so forth. There are also many well-accepted planning techniques. But there are no hard and fast guidelines (like FASB guidelines) that state what good planning is, how it must be done, or when it must be done, if at all. The relative emphasis that the CEO places on any aspect of planning is individual and will reflect the CEO's own sense of priorities and that of the board. The board's role is to review the strategic plan with the CEO and offer counsel. As with the corporate vision, the CEO has full responsibility for the strategic plan.

At least partially reflecting the complexity of the CEO's strategic planning task in a world that is changing faster and faster, the turnover rate for CEOs has increased significantly in the last 15 years. From 1960 to 1964, in a sample of 100 very large corporations, 3.3 percent of the top two executives *resigned annually for reasons other than retirement* (often a euphemism for being fired by the board). From 1965 to 1969, the percentage increased slightly to 3.6 percent annually. From 1970 to 1974, it increased again to 4.1 percent annually. From 1975 to 1979, after the first oil embargo, the country's first taste of double-digit inflation, and the first jolt of Japanese competition, the CEO departure rate more than doubled to 8.6 percent. From 1980 to 1983, it had further mounted to 9.8 percent. Comparable data beyond this period are not available. But with the heavy merger and takeover activity in the mid- and late 1980s, it would seem likely that it has increased rather than decreased.[6]

Rx for Leaders No. 6   Keep in mind the statistics on CEO survival. The board's role with regard to strategic plans is that of review and counsel, not approval. But the board does have the right of approval over the CEO's overall performance. And boards are clearly becoming more demanding.

---

[6]"Turnover at the Top," *Business Week*, December 19, 1983, p. 104.

16

Vision and Values in Other Types of Organizations

Without visions, the people perish.   *Proverbs*

Then the Lord answered me and said:
Write down the vision
Clearly upon the tablets,
so that one can read it readily.
For the vision still has its time,
presses on to fulfillment, and will
not disappoint;
If it delays, wait for it,
it will surely come, it will not be
late.   *The Book of Habakkuk*

Up to this point, I have treated for-profit and not-for-profit institutions as essentially alike in terms of vision, values, and strategic plan development. There are significant differences, however. "The institutional leader...*is primarily an expert in the promotion and protection of values.*"[1] He or she is not a businessperson with a distinctive set of values as a

---

[1]Thomas J. Peters and Robert H. Waterman Jr., *In Search of Excellence*, HarperCollins Publishers, New York, 1982, p. 85, with permission.

197

guide to conduct. *Values are the business.* This is the first and paramount distinction.

Vision and Values in the Not-for-Profit Organization

There are other differences also. Most not-for-profit institutions are characterized by a relatively nonhierarchical organization. The typical for-profit business unit might have anywhere from five to ten organization levels between the leader and the first line manager or professional. The not-for-profit is more often characterized by three or four levels. Furthermore, there are multiple focus points in not-for-profits, e.g., administration, faculty, student body, parents, financial supporters, and friends. The constituencies are not endless, but sometimes they seem that way.

Secondly, this flat and multi-focused organizational structure places an even greater emphasis on the need and search for consensus, inside as well as outside the institution. This can be tedious and time-consuming, but it is also necessary. The preparation time for the first leadership conference in the LCPP process (see Part 2) can often be stretched from 30 to 45 days to 6 to 12 months for the not-for-profit organization. Extensive time may be devoted to the questionnaire and interview process, both individually and in a group context. The most serious problem to avoid is getting stuck there or having difficulty managing and focusing the information gathered. Many not-for-profits are quite fond of information-gathering processes and find closure difficult. Eventually, action must be taken to develop and then realize the organization's vision and values.

A third difference is the need for strategic planning to rationally address a number of areas of continuing and dynamic tension. One kind of tension peculiar to the academic institution is the conflict between respect for tradition and the continuing search for new knowledge. Other clashes exist between the right of the individual and the common good, as well as the search for balance between excellence and the pace and rhythm of institutional life. Finally, emphasis on fundamental values vies with the necessity for financial stewardship as an institution teaches and lives its values. Some feel that the management of these tensions may be the key indicator of the general health of the institution.

Areas of Strength

Drucker says that business can learn much from not-for-profit institutions. "In two areas, strategy and the effectiveness of the board, they are practicing what most American businesses only preach."[2] Drucker's point is well taken. It is also true that not-for-profits can learn much from business. A comparison of not-for-profit and for-profit organizations in regard to vision and strategic planning can be helpful in understanding their relative strengths and weaknesses.

The not-for-profits are generally stronger than the for-profits in terms of the strength of their vision. But the not-for-profits are relatively weaker in terms of most elements of the strategic plan, particularly those having to do with implementation and accountability. I made the point earlier that all visions and strategic plans are value-based and that values are the most fundamental element of the vision. Almost by definition, the not-for-profits are superior in this area. Values are often their main business. I believe they are also superior in the definition of basic mission: They have a very strong and generally well-communicated notion of where they are headed and why.

With regard to long-term goals, the third element of the vision, I don't believe that either type of organization has a distinct advantage. But business does have a distinctive edge in all three areas of the strategic plan. The businessperson's sense of strategy, tactics, and accountability is sharpened and honed from the first day of corporate life. They are more accustomed to task definition, budgets, deadlines, etc. Businesspeople are often recruited at not-for-profit institutions because they possess skills and a good sense of structure.

Institutional Development

The not-for-profit institution's development, or fundraising, function is critical to its survival. A vision and strategic plan that represents a consensus of the key constituents of the institution provides a necessary foundation for the development function. A commitment to make the underlying vision a matter of reality is also required. The development function consists primarily of communicating, shaping, and implementing as opposed to being a visionary driver. The vision should still come from the leadership group of the institution served. Development must maintain a balance between the "grand vision" of the institution and the day-to-day grind for financial survival, establishing a set of internal priorities while remaining open to external priorities. For example, the institution should provide a menu of opportunities for supporters to address, such as a library, housing, recreational facilities, special programs, endowment, etc. The development function also orchestrates celebration of achievement of specific goals and new levels of performance.

[2]Peter F. Drucker, "What Business Can Learn from Nonprofits," *Harvard Business Review*, July-August 1989, p. 88.

Planning Goals

In both types of organizations, the vision and strategic planning process have similar goals. Timothy Sweeney, OSB, Archabbot of St. Meinrad Monastery in Southern Indiana, laid out the following set of planning goals for the monastery, schools, and business that it runs. With very few modifications, they would fit any for-profit organization just as well:

- Growth, especially in quality, of all that St. Meinrad is and does.

- A process whereby the pace and rhythm of the monastic life can be maintained and strengthened by means of integration and prioritizing.

- A uniform format of planning that allows for the diversity of the parts (schools, Abbey Press, etc.) that form the whole we call St. Meinrad.

- A facilitation of the daily decision making in light of the overall direction the plan provides.

- A clarification of the authority of those responsible for decision making.

- An improvement in communication through clearer understanding and a greater commitment.

- An improvement in the proper utilization of our resources.

Rx for Leaders No. 1   Take care in shaping your vision. Then realize your vision with equal emphasis on implementation and accountability.

Vision and Values in the Family Firm

Members of Chicago's billionaire Pritzker family certainly rank among the top businesspeople in the United States. Recently, Robert Pritzker, one of two brothers who lead the family business, has commented, "We don't believe in long-range planning; it's too complicated, and things never work out....We all agreed 15 years ago that we'd meet every Saturday to coordinate what we do. We met that following Saturday, but we haven't done it since."[3] The Pritzker portfolio includes the Hyatt chain of hotels, Marmon Group manufacturing companies, and myriad investments in real estate, lumber, shipping, and financial services. The

---

[3]Steve Weiner, "What, No Strategic Planning Department?," *Forbes*, August 6, 1990, p. 92.

above quotation was taken from a *Forbes* article that appeared in August 1990. The writer concluded, "The moral seems to be that if you are a superb tactician you don't need to worry about strategy."[4]

I believe the lesson to be learned here is quite different. In a family business such as the Pritzkers', run by the two brothers, Robert and Jay, their children, and another generation now coming along, there is a shared heritage that goes far beyond the typical corporate vision statement and strategic plan. They have a family culture, a set of values, mission, and goals that is deeply ingrained in both their conscious and subconscious minds.

While there are many nonfamily executives and managers involved in the business, there is relatively little turnover among the key members. Because the Pritzkers share a common vision and set of values, and because they are gifted in business skills, they are able to skip the formality of written vision statements and strategies and move rather quickly and immediately to tactics.

A recent article on the Cadbury family of Cadbury-Schweppes, PLC makes a somewhat parallel point about family members sharing a sense of visions and values.

> One of the advantages of family members occupying senior management positions, Cadbury said, has been "to bring an understanding of Cadbury values to the company. From its very early days, the firm has been highly progressive in its industrial relations, its human resources policies. We're also known for our integrity and straight dealing, and for our insistence on high quality in everything we do." In fact, one of the earliest statements of Cadbury goals listed the top priority as "the best possible quality—nothing is too good for the public." Although the Cadburys may eventually disappear from the executive suite, Dominic Cadbury expects the family values to survive.[5]

Implicitly shared family values and goals make the business management job inherently easier.

Rx for Leaders No. 2   Build on your shared vision and values, if yours is a family-owned company. You have a head start.

---

[4]Ibid.

[5]Richard Kurovsky, "A Sweet Message for the Global Market," *Stanford Business School Magazine*, October 1989, p. 43., with permission.

Vision and Values in the Smaller Business Firm

Most small businesses do not get any kind of head start. They go through painful business cycles, periods of growth (sometimes rapid) interspersed with periods of struggling for survival. No two small companies are alike, but they do seem to share some common problems and opportunities.

McCoy was founded in 1972 as a furniture installation service company. Today it specializes in furniture and accessories, installation and relocation, service and maintenance, with a staff of over 200. Current sales are approximately $40 million and have grown at an annual rate of 10 to 15 percent over the last five years. McCoy is very growth-oriented but has relatively thin margins and must pay close attention to the bottom line. It has three owners, all of whom are actively involved in the business both operationally and from a policy and goal setting perspective.

An employee survey indicated that the employees liked the company but that communications were weak. Communication problems are not unique to small companies. They are shared by many firms, and the larger the company is, the more serious its problems generally are. The survey also showed some tension between two groups, administration-operations and sales-marketing. Finally, there was a perceived lack of teamwork.

On top of these internal concerns about communications, tension, and lack of teamwork, Thad Minyard, McCoy's president, wanted to get some other people involved in his vision of the future for McCoy. He wanted their personal commitment to help make that vision a reality. The first 20 years of McCoy's corporate life had been quite successful although it had the typical periods of growth and struggling for survival. Minyard's intent was to look out to the next 10 to 20 years.

The McCoy people are much more sensitive to the *customer* and the *quality* of service than most larger companies. Almost all their people deal directly with customers on a daily basis. They hear unfiltered client comments, both negative and positive. The same is true with regard to the quality of the product or service that they deliver. They experience customer feedback directly and are aware of both strengths and deficiencies in the customers' eyes.

Minyard developed the CEO's short list of priorities (see Chap. 11) after the plan had been completed (three to five short-term priorities and three to five long-term priorities). All three of Minyard's short-term priorities involved the customer—customer communications, customer retention, and developing a new customer base. One of the three long-term priorities involved maintaining momentum and increasing the credibility of McCoy's total quality program. The customer and quality focus was strong.

After completing the McCoy vision and strategic plan the core group was asked to identify in a confidential questionnaire what they considered to be the primary accomplishments of the process. The consensus answers were as follows:

- It helped us achieve agreement on shared goals and strategies.
- It developed a team approach in identifying and working together toward corporate goals.
- It enabled us to look at the company as a single entity rather than each department as an isolated group.

When they were asked to identify the critical issues requiring additional work, they focused on the following points: (1) Switch our emphasis to plan implementation, (2) communicate the plan to all employees in the company, and (3) support our plan with appropriate budget allocations.

When asked what should be done to ensure successful plan implementation, almost 75 percent emphasized scheduled follow-up. They suggested that the quarterly review dates discussed in Chap. 12 be set up immediately so that everyone could be there, and there were no excuses for absences. They emphasized the role of the goal champion in monitoring progress on plan tactics. As one person said, "We need to make sure there are victories at that first meeting." This emphasis did not come as a surprise. In the interviews that preceded the three conferences, one person emphasized that "we are really good in making plans, we just don't implement well." They wanted this effort to be successful.

One of the very nice things about the small company is that not just the owners and policy makers of the company are involved in the planning process. Many or most of the first line managers themselves participate. Participation can help increase their knowledge, identification with and commitment to the vision, values, and goals.

Rx for Leaders No. 3   Build on your strengths. In a small company your people are more involved with the customer and the quality of the product. Most of your managers are involved in the development of your vision. Ultimately, your communication task will be simpler.

Vision and Values in Russia

In both for-profit and not-for-profit organizations, large and small, shared values form the foundation for the organizational vision. But is this true outside the western world? Alexei Izyumov, a political analyst and economist at the Soviet Academy of Sciences has written, "Soviet society took only six years of *glasnost* to overcome most of the myths and fetishes of Communism that had been nurtured by the Soviet propaganda machine for nearly 70 years."[6] But this was only the "first step of a badly needed ideological revolution; to complete it, the vacuum created in the minds of millions of Soviets by the swift demolition of old Communist gods has to be filled with a new set of heroes. And that seems a more difficult task."[7]

Izyumov says that what's needed is a "massive educational campaign to fill the minds of disenchanted Soviets with the values and ideas that helped the nation of the civilized world to survive and prosper."[8] These values will provide the necessary foundation for the rest of the vision to take shape.

A Visual Summary

All institutions, large or small, for-profit or not-for-profit, public or private, live in an increasingly competitive environment that is rapidly becoming global. Perhaps the best visual summary of the competitive message of this book is a recent advertisement by one of the baby Bell companies, U.S. West. The ad shows a large group of cowboys riding across a very dry and open plain on a beautiful day. The leader and one or two other cowboys can be seen clearly. The rest are shrouded in dust. The theme is very appropriate: "If you don't make dust, you eat dust."

Rx for Leaders No. 4   Make dust or eat it! Renew or perish. Your performance must always be evaluated relative to your competitors.

Some Critical Prescriptions

As pointed out in the introduction, this book is specifically directed to active leaders and their leadership groups. Any final attempt to summarize

[6]Richard Lourie, *Predicting Russia's Future* (Whittle Direct Books, 1991), p. 80.
[7]Ibid.
[8]Ibid.

its contents would have to be based on its more critical "Rx for Leaders." Ten of the most important are repeated below:

- Make your vision as clear as your profit goals. Profit alone is not enough to motivate your people. Expand the scope of your vision to address more of the whole person.

- Values are meant to stir the heart, not close the mind. Be open to the important values of your people.

- Get your people to focus on aspirations for the future. These aspirations can grab the organization and become the catapult to business success.

- Participate in and shape the key elements of your corporation's vision. Manage and guide the debate among your senior managers. Ultimately, you must be the architect and master builder of your vision and strategic plan.

- Listen to your people throughout this whole process. Listening to them will make them stronger. It doesn't diminish your leadership; it strengthens it.

- Make certain you communicate your vision and shared values to everyone in the company. Consensus and commitment generally fall off the deeper you go in the organization.

- Pick a path to success that suits your company and be tenacious. There are a lot of paths toward excellence, but they all seem to include quality and a high regard for your people.

- Pay your people a little better and yourself a little less and you'll probably build a better team.

- Delegate everything else if you have to but don't delegate the responsibility for charting the corporation's future. Gaining acceptance of the corporate vision is your responsibility.

- Make dust or eat it! Renew or perish. Your performance must always be evaluated relative to your competitors.

Bibliography

Bass, Bernard. *Leadership and Performance Beyond Expectations,* Free Press, New York, 1985.

Belasco, James A. *Teaching the Elephant to Dance,* Crown Publishers, New York, 1990.

Bennis, Warren, and Burt Nanus. *Leaders: The Strategy For Taking Charge,* Harper Collins, New York, 1985.

Blanchard, Kenneth, and Norman Vincent Peale. *The Power of Ethical Management,* William Morrow, New York, 1988.

Bloom, Allan. *The Closing of the American Mind,* Simon & Schuster, New York, 1987.

Burrough, Bryan, and John Helyar. *Barbarians at the Gate: The Fall of RJR Nabisco,* Harper & Row, New York, 1990.

DePree, Max. *Leadership is an Art,* Doubleday, New York, 1989.

Drucker, Peter F. *Management: Tasks, Practices, Responsibilities,* Harper & Row, New York, 1974.

Durant, Will and Ariele. *The Lessons of History,* Simon & Schuster, New York, 1968.

Follett, Mary Parker. *Dynamic Administration,* Harper & Row, New York, 1941.

Gardner, John W. *Excellence,* Harper & Row, New York, 1961.

Gardner, John W. *On Leadership,* The Free Press, New York, 1990.

Garfield, Charles. *Peak Performers,* Avon Books, New York, 1986.

Greenleaf, Robert. *Servant Leadership,* Paulist Press, Mahwah, N. J., 1979.

Hesburgh, Theodore. M. *God, Country, Notre Dame,* Doubleday, New York, 1990.

Hickman, Craig R., and Michael A. Silva. *Creating Excellence: Managing Corporate Culture, Strategy, and Change in the New Age,* New American Library, New York, 1984.

Kanter, Rosabeth Moss. *The Change Masters,* Simon & Schuster, New York, 1983.

Kanter, Rosabeth Moss. *Men and Women of the Corporation,* Basic Books, New York, 1977.

Levinson, Harry, and Stuart Rosenthal. *CEO,* Basic Books, New York, 1984.

Pascale, Richard Tanner, and Anthony G. Athos. *The Art of Japanese Management,* Simon & Schuster, New York, 1981.

Peters, Thomas J., and Robert H. Waterman. *In Search of Excellence,* Harper & Row, New York, 1982.

Peters, Tom. *Thriving on Chaos,* Alfred A. Knopf, New York, 1987.

Rodgers, William. *Think,* Stein and Day, New York, 1969.

Shames, Laurence. *The Hunger For More: Searching for Values in an Age of Greed*, Times, New York, 1989.

Sonnenfeld, Jeffrey. *The Hero's Farewell*, Oxford University Press, New York, 1988.

Tichy, Noel M., and Mary Anne Devanna. *The Transformational Leader*, John Wiley & Sons, New York, 1986.

Tregoe, Benjamin B., et al. *Vision in Action: Putting a Winning Strategy to Work*, Simon & Schuster, New York, 1989.

Waterman, Robert H. *The Renewal Factor: How the Best Get and Keep the Competitive Edge*, Bantam Books, New York, 1987.

Watson, Thomas J. Jr. *Father Son & Co.: My Life at IBM and Beyond*, Bantam Books, New York, 1990.

Zaleznik, Abraham. *The Managerial Mystique: Restoring Leadership in Business*, Harper & Row, New York, 1989.

Index